Coasts and Beaches

---

CONTEMPORARY
SCIENCE
PAPERBACKS
34

J. A. STEERS M.A.

*Professor Emeritus of Geography, University of Cambridge*

# Coasts and Beaches

OLIVER & BOYD  *Edinburgh*

OLIVER AND BOYD LTD
Tweeddale Court Edinburgh 1

First published 1969
© 1969 J. A. Steers

05 001743 8

Set in Times New Roman and printed in
Great Britain by Hazell Watson & Viney Ltd
Aylesbury, Bucks

# Preface

In recent years there has been a considerable increase in the attention given to coasts. This has come about in several ways, the chief of which are: the consequences of the great storm surge of 1953, the ever-increasing demand for coastal holidays, and the large number of scientific studies of the coast. In this book I have tried to give the general reader, and those who seek an introduction to coastal studies, some notion of the width and ramifications of the subject. Workers in many different fields are vitally concerned with the coast in one way or another and it is advantageous that, as far as possible, their different approaches and points of view should be understood. In some 40 000 words this cannot be achieved with any completeness, but I hope that the subjects discussed and the examples, taken from several countries, will allow the reader to expand his interest both from more detailed works and also by making his own observations on a piece of coast. The nature of, and the forces working upon, adjacent stretches of coast that may appear to be almost identical, are not the same. On a straight open coast conditions may be very similar for some distance, but they are changed if, for example, the trend or the gradient of the beach alters even slightly, or if man has erected a single groyne or other form of sea defence. Moreover, on many parts of the coast change is relatively quick: the alterations in spits and bars, the upward growth of salt marshes, and the recession of boulder clay cliffs show this most clearly. These changes can all be measured, and the more accurate accounts of gain and loss we have the better. Anyone who visits a part of the coast at fairly frequent intervals, and who observes it carefully, is in a position to make useful and even valuable contributions to our knowledge of coastal processes.

Increasing pressure on the coast of any country for holidays or any other purpose inevitably raises great problems concerning the right use of the coast. This is not a book about planning, but everyone should ponder this aspect of the subject. Not only in Britain is the coast one of the most beautiful and interesting features of the country. Yet in order to preserve this beauty the millions who want to – and should – visit it must appreciate that conservation means the right use of the coast for the benefit of all; it does not mean indiscriminate development of any sort, nor does it mean prohibition to use the coast and enjoy it.

I am grateful to all those whose writings have helped me to make this book; acknowledgement is made in appropriate places to them and to those who have allowed me to use their photographs. To Mr B. W. Sparks I am indebted for reading the typescript and for making many helpful suggestions.

                                                              J. A. STEERS

# Contents

# 1. Introductory

Most people in the British Isles are acquainted with some part or parts of the coastline, although it is probably true to say that a considerable proportion of them know mainly the built-up areas. Others who visit the wilder parts are familiar with some of the great beauty and variety which characterise our coast. Few, however, think of the coast from the point of view of its evolution and, except in a very general way, probably do not make comparisons, from the physical or natural history point of view, of one part with another. Those who know the coast well realise how good it is, and how fast some parts of it are being spoiled, and they know too that there is more variation in the scenery of our coast than that of probably any other country in the world. This is a bold statement to make, but it is justified if we appreciate only a few quite general points about the structure of Britain.

First of all, Britain contains rocks of almost all ages, from the early pre-Cambrian gneisses of north-western Scotland or the ancient rocks of the Mona complex of Anglesey to the recent boulder clays which form so much of the coast of eastern England. The most casual visitor will notice marked differences between the cliffs of Land's End, Pembrokeshire, Skye, Caithness, Kent and East Anglia. What adds so much to the beauty of the coast is not only the fact of the large number of rocks of different ages which are seen in the cliffs, but also the extremely different nature of the rocks – chalk, limestones, sandstones, basalts, granite and clays – and the fact that many of these rocks are folded and faulted, so that the sea, eating into them, accentuates these details and forms caves, stacks, narrow gullies and steep cliffs. Elsewhere we find flat coasts, some of which are amongst the most beautiful

we have. Consider such examples as the magnificent marshland coast of north Norfolk; the fine dunes and associated
features on the Moray Firth between Nairn and Elgin, and
also around the north-east corner of Aberdeenshire; the
extensive areas of dunes on both sides of the Bristol Channel;
and the coastal plain of Hampshire and Sussex, much of
which is now built upon, but of which there are still unspoiled
parts around the Solent, Spithead and Chichester.

If we glance at our coast from a more technical point of
view, we shall also notice great variations between different
parts, some of which are not at all distant from one another.
South-eastern England is known to millions. Its physical
form and the variation of its coastal scenery are largely
dependent upon its geological structure, the main trends of
which are relatively easy to follow.

The chalk is folded and now makes two main ridges. The
North Downs run through Kent and reach the sea to form
cliffs at and on either side of the North Foreland. The Isle of
Thanet forms a separate and distinct chalk area. The South
Downs make the inner boundary of the Sussex coastal plain
and reach the sea at Seaford, the Seven Sisters and Beachy
Head. If we reconstruct the chalk we should find that it once
formed a great arch, the middle part of which has been worn
away so that older rocks are exposed within forming the core
of the Weald, and giving the cliffs at Hastings and those
behind Romney Marsh. The chalk of the North Downs dips (or
slopes) northwards under the Thames, which is lined with
newer rocks which make the easily eroded shores of the Isle of
Sheppey and the lowlying coast of Essex. The chalk of the
South Downs dips to the south, and reappears locally in the
central ridge of the Isle of Wight, the ridge running from
Culver Cliff to the Needles. This ridge is also part of an arch,
the southern limb of which appears around St Boniface Down
in the south of the island. Between the South Downs and the
central ridge of the Isle of Wight is the Sussex coastal plain, the
Spithead and Solent, and the lowlying coasts associated with
these features. These coasts are all formed of easily eroded
rocks, and in the sheltered bays and inlets salt marshes have

grown, especially the great spreads of Spartina grass in
Southampton Water and farther west in Poole Harbour. If we
look at a geological or at a physical map we note that the
western end of this the Isle of Wight ridge, and the chalk ridge
which runs west to east in the Isle of Purbeck and ends eastwards in Handfast Point and Old Harry Rocks, face one
another. They were once joined across the bay in which
Bournemouth now stands. The river Frome, which reaches
salt-water in Poole Harbour, and enters the main sea between
the Sandbanks and South Haven peninsulas, both sand
formations, once continued as a river inside the Purbeck-Wight
ridge and then via the Solent and Spithead, after which it
turned south and east to join a trunk stream running east to
west along the then exposed floor of the English Channel. In
brief, in this part of England we have a coast which, structurally, is controlled by the folding of rocks of Mesozoic age to
give the chalk ridges and intervening lower ground of *older*
rocks between the Downs, and *newer* rocks between the
South Downs and the isles of Wight and Purbeck. Later it has
been submerged to give drowned features such as the harbours near Portsmouth and Chichester, the Solent, Spithead,
Southampton Water and Poole Harbour; it has also suffered
erosion; the Purbeck-Wight ridge, for example, did not disappear only by submergence, but by sea erosion and river erosion.
The small rivers that today flow northwards from the Isle of
Wight are similar to others that at one time drained the con-
necting ridge. The eastern and western Yars almost make
three islands of the Isle of Wight, and would do so completely
if there were a little further submergence. But at some time
emergence, or a fall of sea-level, must have taken place to give
the flat coastal plain of west Sussex, and also the remains of a
raised beach we find (or used to find before being obscured by
buildings) at Brighton, and the higher beaches, some way inland, near Slindon and Goodwood. What is more, we must
also take into consideration the wide Chalk platforms, cut by
the sea, and now exposed at low water around parts of the Isle
of Thanet – a true island before the entrances, near Reculver
and Richborough, of the channel which formerly separated it

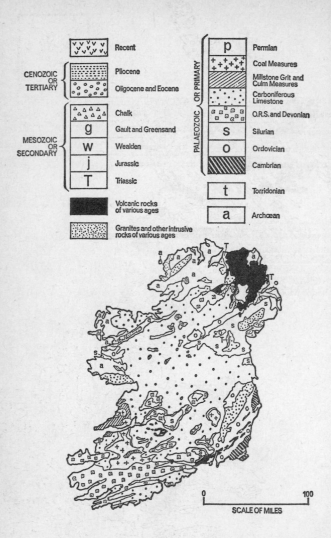

| | Recent |
|---|---|
| | Pliocene |
| | Oligocene and Eocene |

CENOZOIC OR TERTIARY

| | Chalk |
|---|---|
| g | Gault and Greensand |
| w | Wealden |
| j | Jurassic |
| T | Triassic |

MESOZOIC OR SECONDARY

| | Volcanic rocks of various ages |
|---|---|
| | Granites and other intrusive rocks of various ages |

| p | Permian |
|---|---|
| | Coal Measures |
| | Millstone Grit and Culm Measures |
| | Carboniferous Limestone |
| | O.R.S. and Devonian |
| s | Silurian |
| o | Ordovician |
| | Cambrian |

PALAEOZOIC OR PRIMARY

| t | Torridonian |
|---|---|
| a | Archœan |

SCALE OF MILES
0 100

Fig. 1. *Outline geological map of the British Isles.*

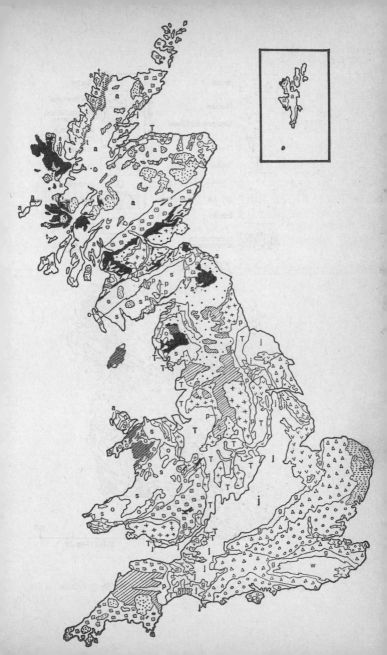

from the mainland were finally blocked by natural accretion and other causes.

This rather long, but nevertheless over-simplified outline of some of the changes which have helped to form the coast of part of south-eastern England shows how difficult, in fact impossible, it is to give a simple answer to 'explain' a piece of coast. It is unnecessary to describe many examples in this chapter, but brief reference to the west coast of Scotland is of interest. In Skye, Mull, Staffa and many other smaller islands there are great sheets of basalt and dolerite which were erupted from fissures in Tertiary times. Associated with them are certain great centres of former volcanic eruption, including the western part of the Ardnamurchan peninsula, the Cuillin Hills of Skye, the high ground of central Mull and, somewhat farther afield, parts of Arran and St Kilda. The igneous rocks were all either erupted or poured out on a land surface – old soils are often visible between lava flows – which later collapsed to give a beginning to the intricate outlines of the Hebridean landscape today. All this igneous area lies between two areas of very ancient rock, the pre-Cambrian gneisses of the Outer Hebrides and the corresponding gneisses and the later, but still pre-Cambrian, Torridon Sandstones of the mainland. This region was glaciated and, especially on the mainland, we find the sea-lochs or fiords the appearance of which owes much to the work of ice, although (see p. 17) their origin can by no means always be explained in this way, and a magnificent suite of raised beaches, all of which have suffered some degree of tilting since their formation. On the other hand, whilst all this was happening in western Scotland, the East Anglian coast was sinking and soft sandy rocks, called crags, were accumulating. These were often covered by glacial deposits and later all were raised up and now often form low cliffs subject to serious erosion.

If we keep these examples in mind, and remember that a great deal of detail has been omitted, we shall see how difficult it is to describe coastal types at all adequately. It is, however, useful and helpful to visualise types of coast, and even to make classifications of coasts. We shall not do this here, since to do so adequately would involve a discussion of existing classifications (page 12). These are valuable, but should not be regarded as in any sense final or complete. Classifications are in themselves useful exercises, and they enable their makers and those who study them to criticise them and by so doing to think more comprehensively about coastal problems in general. But in this little book it will be helpful to glance at a physical globe and notice some of the major types of coast-line. In so doing we shall not attempt to simplify matters. but rather the reverse, in order to call attention to the complexity of coasts. Moreover, no attempt will be made to cover the whole globe or every major coastal type.

In high latitudes, fiord coasts usually are best developed on the west side of land masses along which there are mountains or high ground. British Columbia, Scotland, Norway, Green-land (east and west coasts), southern Chile, the south-western part of New Zealand and parts of the Antarctic continent afford superb examples. But fiords are not simple! We may well agree that their major outlines – steep walls, flattish floors, threshold between the fiord and the open sea, the rectangular branching and other features – are best explained by glacial erosion, but glacial erosion acting upon what? The high ground is necessary for the accumulation of snow and ice-sheets and the formation of glaciers. In many instances the glaciers followed pre-existing river valleys. These valleys themselves followed either lines of weakness, or lines of low ground (also probably associated with weakness) in the rocks. Some of these valleys may, in the first place, have been out-lined by faulting, some may have been rifts, i.e. narrow strips let down between parallel faults. Almost all have, since the retreat of the ice, been submerged and usually there may have been more than one up or down movement. The local pattern of fiord coasts will depend on the nature of the original moun-tain system. In Scandinavia the mountains are ancient and the fiords are really cut in a high plateau; in New Zealand and British Columbia the mountains are newer, and have a far less plateau-like aspect. Usually, too, fiord coasts are fringed by numerous islands, varying from the low flat skerryguard of

Scandinavia to the much higher islands of Chile. Nevertheless
– *plus ça change, plus c'est la même chose* – no two fiord coasts
are exactly alike, and we shall see that what is true of them is

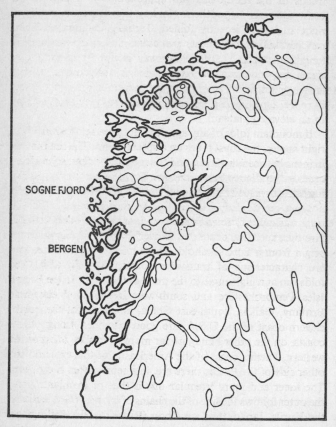

Fig. 2. *The fiord coast near Bergen, Norway.*

also true of all other types of coast. In contrast to the fiord
coasts are the coasts of, for example, Sweden and eastern
Scotland. Both are formed of resistant rocks; both were
glaciated; both are drowned, but in eastern Scotland and in

the Baltic the coasts are relatively low and the true sea fiord is absent.

In fiord areas it is generally true that the major structural trends of the mountains run approximately parallel to the coast, although in southern Norway they are more nearly at right angles. If recently folded, Tertiary, mountains chains run parallel to the coast, the coast is sometimes called a longitudinal coast. Strictly Norway is not in this category since the folding of the mountains is Caledonian, a very ancient mountain system, and the mountains now no longer have the appearance of recently folded ranges, but rather that of an elevated plateau.

If mountain folds of any age run out to sea approximately at right angles, the coast takes on a special form. The sea runs up in inlets between the folds, and the mountains themselves form capes or headlands between them. These inlets are very unlike fiords; they usually widen and deepen seawards and there is nothing resembling a threshold. In certain cases a bar or ridge of sand may form in them and, as in south-west Ireland, give the superficial effect of a barrier, but it is of very different origin from a fiord theshold. These inlets are called rias and are characteristic of transverse coasts, those in which the folds run at a high angle to the trend of the coast. In the British Isles, Pembrokeshire and south-west Ireland, and elsewhere Brittany, Galicia, south-east China, and parts of the north-eastern coast of the U.S.A. are good examples. Longitudinal coasts, on the other hand, are far more extensive. Most of the western, Pacific, coast of the Americas is of this type; on the other side of the Pacific there are, in a sense, often two coasts. The inner and more irregular one is that of mainland Asia; the outer follows the line of the chains of islands, the Aleutians, the Kurils, Japan, the Loo Choo (Riu Kiu), the Philippines, possibly through New Guinea to the Solomons and New Hebrides, and even New Zealand. These are all areas of recent folding, and on the outer, eastern, sides are often fringed by great deeps.

Other major lines of coast are plateaux, which may or may not be fringed by reefs or sandy beaches. Nevertheless,

structurally the plateau is the significant feature. Much of the
south Atlantic and the Indian Oceans is faced by coasts of this
type. Other long stretches of coast are flat and often alluvial in
origin. Much of the north Siberian coast appears to be of this

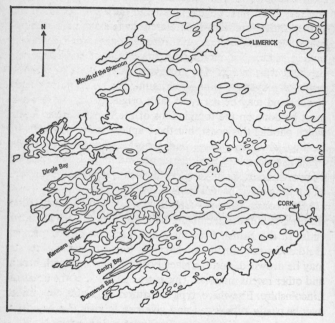

Fig. 3. *The ria coast of south-western Eire.*

nature. In other parts of the world there are extensive alluvial
coasts formed largely of deposits brought down by rivers; the
coast between the Amazon and the Orinoco is of this type, as
indeed may be that of northern Siberia. Extensive alluvial
coasts are formed when great rivers build deltas, as in the
Gulf of Mexico, Egypt and many other places. But in what
category should the east coast of the United States be placed?
It is a low coast, along the outer margin of which are a number
of extensive sand islands, or barrier beaches. Inland the
coastal strip is bordered by the fall-line, an old cliff. The

coastal strip itself is a raised sea floor, later partially drowned to give the long and intricately branching inlets such as the mouths of the Chesapeake and Delaware, and Pamlico Sound.

Some coasts may be largely determined by faults. There are local examples in New Zealand (see p. 79). The great San Andreas fault runs roughly parallel to the Pacific coast of the United States and locally is closely associated with marked coastal features, Bolinas and Tomales Bays, and the coastal outline as far north as Punta Arena. South of San Francisco the fault runs inland. The great earthquake of 1906 was the result of movement along this fault. The coast of northern Queensland may be partly of fault origin. Much more work must be done on the foundations of the Great Barrier Reefs which parallel this coast, but there appear to be evidences of faulting which may have had a profound influence on the trend of the coast. Coral coasts are discussed in Chapter 6; from our present point of view, the fact that a coast is border-ed by fringing or barrier reefs is insignificant.

Many coasts are formed in areas of glacial deposits. Often the sea has cut into them and made long lies of easily eroded cliffs. In the British Isles there are magnificent examples in Holderness and north-east Norfolk. Sometimes these coasts may be drowned, and the glacial deposits covered with beach and other recent material. This is true of much of the coast of Lincolnshire. Elsewhere, typical features of glacial deposition may be partly submerged and give rise to such characteristic areas as the drumlins in Clew Bay (western Ireland) or Nantas-ket beach and the adjacent coast of the north-eastern United States.

Some coasts appear to have been stable over long periods of geological time; most, however, are associated with less stable regions. But whilst such a general distinction is valuable, both types have been affected by sea-level, eustatic, movements. It is shown in Chapter 5 that sea-level fluctuated greatly with the waxing and waning of the great ice-sheets. Since the final melting of the ice, there must have been a rise in sea-level and excepting possibly a few places where local upward movements of some magnitude have taken place, the effect of this rise of sea-level has been a drowning of the coast, both in stable and unstable regions. Stability over long periods of time is difficult to prove, however. Coasts around volcanic areas are usually highly unstable and liable to movements of one sort or another; the outpouring of volcanic ash and dust may have more than merely local effects.

It will be abundantly clear that there are many ways of looking at coasts, and all those who have devised classifications have based them on different criteria. Suess, many years ago, was chiefly concerned with the profound differences between Atlantic and Pacific types; Richthofen emphasised such features as fiords, rias and longitudinal and transverse coasts. D. W. Johnson, in 1919, differentiated submerged and emerged coasts, and also neutral and compound ones. In 1948 F. P. Shepard took as his main headings Primary or Youthful coasts shaped either by terrestrial erosion or deposition, and Secondary or Mature coasts shaped by marine erosion or deposition. C. A. Cotton (1952) separated various categories in stable and unstable regions. H. Valentin (1952) based his views on prograding (i.e. growing forward) and retreating coasts, distinguishing many separate types. G. T. McGill (1958) had a more elaborate scheme in which he discussed the principal land-shaping agents (ice, water, wind, etc.) on low-lands and uplands of varying structure.

All of these classifications are useful and interesting, but none is completely adequate, and the chief value of any one is that it provokes thought, and may therefore lead to the development of new and interesting ideas. The point is that since no two coasts are identical, classification cannot be truly comprehensive.

# 2. Waves and Tidal Currents: Movements of Beach Material

There is no doubt that the most effective agent at work on the coast is wave action. In the past, current action used to be emphasised; it is certainly an important factor and must be considered in relation to wave action.

Anyone standing on the beach, or still better on a high cliff or pier, will notice that the nature of the waves approaching a shore varies with the local conditions and the weather. In calm weather there may be little or no wave action; on the other hand a long swell may be rolling into the beaches, the product of some distant storm. If the wind is offshore, wave action on the beach may be absent or negligible. An onshore wind will have different effects according to the direction, relative to the beach, from which it blows. If it is directly on-shore, the waves break parallel to the beach; it it is oblique then the waves also approach obliquely and, as it were, run along the beach. In a storm or as the result of a storm, there may be more than one set of waves. But on an ordinary shelving beach, no matter from what direction the waves come, the shallowing will retard the waves; their crests will travel forward quicker than the troughs, and sooner or later will fall forward and send a rush of water up the beach. This is the swash. If a wave approaches obliquely, the part which first feels the effect of shallower water is retarded, and the waves 'swing round' so that the outer parts catch up with those nearer the beach, and at any point the waves break so that the swash, instead of running directly up the beach, follows a slanting path. But in this case, just as when the wave breaks parallel to the beach, the swash when it ceases to run up the

beach retreats *directly* down to the water again. This is sometimes called the backwash.

This oblique approach of the swash is of immense importance in coastal engineering. If you watch while waves of this
sort are breaking, you will notice that sand and stones are
carried slantwise up the beach by the swash. Those particles
at and close to the margin of the swash will probably be left
stranded; those lower down are carried directly back to the sea
by the backwash. They have thus advanced laterally along the
beach. Each wave has a similar effect; with a rising tide more
and more of the beach is affected and in consequence a vast
amount of material is moved. If, because of a change of wind,
the waves affecting a beach later come in from the opposite
direction much of the material is moved back. On open coasts,

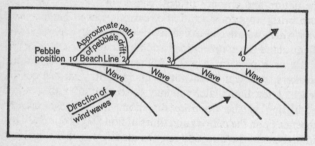

Fig. 4. *Diagram illustrating beach-drifting.*

however, there is usually a prevailing wind, and despite occasional changes, the movement of material is primarily in one
direction (Fig. 4).

Another important factor must be considered here. The size
and frequency of waves approaching a beach depends much
upon the amount of open water facing that beach. On the East
Anglian coast of England, for example, the greatest amount of
open water is to the north and north-east, and winds blowing
from these directions have the greatest fetch relative to the
coast, and sometimes even if the wind immediately at the
coast is offshore, the waves approaching the beach may be
coming in from the open ocean. If, for the moment, we think

of one major direction of approach – this is perhaps an over-simplification – the effect of waves on the coast will depend upon the angle at which they approach any part of it. On the East Anglian coast waves approaching from the north-east are likely to cause a swash that will move particles westwards along the coast of north Norfolk and southwards along the coast south of, say, Yarmouth. There are, of course, complications which will vary greatly with local features.

Nevertheless, this process, called beach-drifting, is all-important. It is responsible for the deflection of river mouths, for the building of bars across harbours, and for the piling up of beach material on the up-drift sides of groynes and break-waters.

Before discussing various means of measuring or estimating the nature and amount of drift caused in this way, we must turn briefly to a consideration of current action. The currents with which we are concerned are nearly always tidal currents. If you stand on an open beach and throw into the sea a corked bottle or a piece of wood, provided that it is clear of the breakers, you will often notice that it drifts parallel to the beach. A few hours later you may notice that a floating object is drifting in the opposite direction. The change usually depends upon the periods and times of flood and ebb tide. To a limited extent the direction may be modified by the wind, but apart from exceptional conditions, the wind will only modify the surface current. The time of change of current direction usually, but not necessarily, corresponds with that of ebb and flood. But at flood, i.e. high water, much more of the beach is covered than at low water, and consequently if the flood current moves in an easterly direction, its effects are not likely to be obliterated on the higher parts of the beach by the ebb current which will only affect the lower part. This phenomenon will be more noticeable if the tidal range is considerable. But what are the effects? One can perhaps most easily appreciate their general nature when bathing at a time when small waves are approaching the beach. If you stand in water about four to five feet deep you will find yourself buoyed up when a wave approaches; if you are standing on sand you may feel that it is disturbed about your feet. If at the same time a tidal current is running parallel to the beach (you will soon discover this for yourself if you float) the sand that is stirred up around your feet is carried a little sideways with the current. In rough weather the effect is naturally greater. Much, perhaps all, will be brought back during the ebb. If, however, one current (often, but not always, the flood current) is stronger than the other, then the general movement of material will be in one direction.

If we now consider the combined effects of beach-drifting (wave action) and current action it is easy to see that vast amounts of material may be transported along a coast. On many British beaches we shall also notice that the upper part of the beach is of shingle, whilst lower down it is sandy. This sorting is again the work of waves, and it is significant that since the upper part of the beach is mainly covered at high water, then the shingle is moved mainly at that time. But in storms, when a great amount of water is piled up on the beach, the shingle is often combed down, and then much of it may be moved at lower stages of the tide. In the course of a few days, however, the shingle is usually pushed back again to the top of the beach.

The importance of lateral movements of beach material has long been recognised, but in recent years the significance has been much more fully appreciated, and Zenkovich, who has done much work on Russian beaches, speaks of sediment-streams. In their movement along a coast they may cause wide accumulations on the upstream side of a headland or cape. Elsewhere they may even denude a part of the coast. More-over, they inevitably alter the submarine profile, and so cause waves to break farther out or closer in to the beach according to local circumstances.

On a coast where there are cliffs of resistant rock and many inlets, small and big, enclosed between headlands, the lateral displacement of beach material is restricted. Each re-entrant may contain a beach at its head. This is a relatively stable feature; it may be swept out in storms, but sooner or later it is rebuilt. The material of which it is formed may be quite local in origin; on an irregular coast little, if any, continuous drift takes place along the coast as a whole.* In inlets which run well back into the land, a beach or bar may form some way from the head of the bay. If the sediment stream along the margins of the bay is arrested by the shallowing of the bay or for some other reason, it may lead to the formation of a mid-bay bar. A good example is to be seen in Cemlyn Bay in Anglesey.

If there is a coast broken by headlands and inlets, and if the headlands are built of rock that yields relatively easily to erosion, they will be cut back, and the material thus added to the debris-stream will be carried along the coast, and begin to build spits across the mouths of inlets and rivers. In a later chapter we shall examine the nature of such features in greater detail; here it is sufficient to say that their free ends usually turn inward, and that they are features, especially in the early stages of their growth, much subject to alterations, often profound in storms and times of rough weather.

It is, however, all too easy to over-simplify coastal pheno-mena. In Chapter 3 reference is made to Orford Ness. Its structure and what is known of its growth from historical records show that it has unquestionably extended southwards from near Aldeburgh to its present end not far from Bawdsey. But just south of Aldeburgh there are now a number of groynes built to halt the erosion taking place at the south end of that town. In the big surge of 1953 waves over-topped this part of the beach and the water reached the river Alde, but the shingle ridge, although flattened, was not severed. The beach at this part now has a somewhat artificial appearance since the shingle was reincorporated into the beach by mechanical methods. But, allowing for this type of change, it is often noticeable that the groynes indicate, by the piling up of shingle on their southern sides, a reverse, south to north, movement of beach material. This is the result of south-easterly winds, and

* Material does move around headlands and rocky peninsulas, but it is only occasionally that such movements can be proved. Trask showed that material moves around the headlands of Point Arguello and Con-ception on the coast of California. These headlands plunge into deep water, and only small isolated beaches occur along this stretch of coast.

if they blow for some time, and if they are succeeded by calm weather before northerly winds return, they may be responsible for a reversal of movement involving considerable quantities of shingle. Because of the groynes much of this may stay until washed out by a storm. Some years ago (see p. 25) experiments with radioactive tracers were made along the southern end of the Orford spit. Tracers put down on the beach in January 1957, during light south-easterly winds, began to move northwards. After four weeks one pebble was 1¼ miles north of the place where it was put down; the average movement was about 600 yards. In the fifth week gentle north-east winds set in, and the movement of pebbles was immediately reversed, some not only reaching the end of the spit but even to the shingle knolls which usually form in the haven's mouth, and some pebbles travelled to Shingle Street. At Blakeney Point as a result of some careful experiments, it has been suggested that the general movement of pebbles is to the east, against the apparent direction of growth of the shingle spit. There is no doubt that reverse movements can and do take place, but the nature and physical form of the spit clearly points to a westward growth, and all that is known of the evolution of the spit from historical records is in agreement with this view.* The other objection rests on the supply of shingle. There is, to all intends and purposes, no shingle available for this purpose to the west of Blakeney Far Point. The amount on the coast between there and Wells is limited, and for the most part well back from any wave action that could effectively help to feed Blakeney. To maintain that the eastward movement must be sustained by the waste of Blakeney Point itself is difficult, since the amount of shingle at the Point is limited, and there is no evidence for postulating that large volumes of shingle existed in past times somewhere near the present headland. It is extremely unlikely that the present shingle, which still bends inwards and from time to time adds to the Far Point, could have supplied the great volumes that

---

* See *Trans. Inst. Br. Geogr.*, 1964, and Steers *The Coastline of England and Wales,* 2nd ed. 1964, p. 657, for a full discussion of this interesting matter.

make up the spit which runs for about eight miles before it joins the cliffs at Weybourne.

There is, however, another factor to consider on the north Norfolk coast. A general glance at the one-inch map shows that although the harbour mouths at Blakeney and Brancaster Staithe are at first deflected westwards, they nevertheless turn eastwards in the sand flats. Thus there appear to be two movements to consider: a westward deflection of the upper shingle beaches brought about by wave action, and an eastward deflection in the sand flats lower down which may well be the combined result of current and wave action. In general terms these matters have been supported by observation and elementary experiments, but a full analysis would be of interest.

What has been said so far applies more particularly to beaches in the British Isles. But they are perhaps somewhat anomalous. In many parts of the world extensive beaches are not backed by shingle, and to an Englishman look unfamiliar and, at first sight, somewhat more attractive. The same processes operate upon them, but it by no means follows that beach-drifting is so marked a phenomenon as in many places around our own coasts. In Australia, for example, Bird has argued that the shaping of beaches which are exposed to ocean swells is the result of wave refraction as the swell approaches the coast. 'The effect of ocean swells is thus to modify the configuration of the coast, simplifying the irregular outlines produced by recent submergence into a succession of curved sandy shores between protruding rocky headlands, as on the coast of New South Wales. If the shoreline is less sharply curved than the approaching swell, lateral currents are generated which move the sand to the centre of the bay, prograding it until it fits the outline of the arriving swell. It is a process of natural adjustment, for as the sea floor is smoothed by erosion and deposition, wave refraction becomes less intense, and the outlines of beaches correspondingly less sharply curved.' (E. C. Bird, *Coastal Land-forms*, p. 70.) These beaches are formed entirely of sand; that the same processes would apply if there were also shingle is certainly true, but it is not easy to find examples of long beaches on which there is an abundance of shingle. It is probably correct to say that most shingle beaches are formed along coasts of formerly glaciated areas. In Britain, on the south and east coasts, most of the shingle (often > 90%) is flint. This is not all derived directly from the chalk – probably only a small proportion comes immediately from that source – but from glacial drifts, river gravels, solifluction and other glacial or peri-glacial deposits. Locally, shingle is directly derived from the adjacent cliffs; the limestone pebbles at the southern end of the Chesil Beach come from Portland Island; the Liassic pebbles on the Glamorganshire coast are directly derived from the cliffs, but on the south coast on the Lleyn peninsula probably most of the pebbles come from glacial deposits. This is, of course, true of the beaches of Holderness and the piece of coast between Sheringham and Happisburgh in Norfolk. But it is most improbable that all the pebbles on those two beaches are so derived. The floor of the North Sea is shallow; over much of it there are abundant glacial deposits. The question thus arises: Can a beach be fed directly from the sea floor?

There is little doubt that sand can be driven inshore by wave action. This has been demonstrated in wave tanks. Zenkovich maintains that the material of certain shell beaches must be derived from offshore: there is no other source. In Skye and one or two other places in Scotland, there are small white beaches formed almost wholly of byozoans, lime-secreting organisms which live on the sea bed. Around coral islands (see Chapter 6) a good deal of coral shingle is driven directly on shore. But the direct supply of shingle from the sea floor presents difficulties. Before discussing these, however, it is pertinent to note that some beach shingle may be very old, even fossil, in the sense that it is not all of present-day age. It was noted above that much is derived from glacial deposits, but not necessarily deposits that are now being eroded by the sea. These, in England, are almost certainly too limited in extent to supply all the shingle present. On the other hand (see Chapter 5), we know that in terms of geological time it was only yesterday that the North Sea floor and the floors of other shallow seas around our coasts were wholly or largely uncovered. When they began to fill up, the waves in the expanding seas would work on the floor deposits and, just as on a modern beach, begin to sort them out. Shingle could in this way be driven landward by the rising sea. This has been suggested by Baden Powell in order to account for the vast amount of stones in the Chesil Beach. This process, involving several thousands of years, has undoubtedly taken place, but it is by no means certain that shingle, at its present size, could last this length of time on account of the constant wear and tear to which it must have been subjected. Are we to suppose the process started on large boulders which have generally been reduced in size? Whatever the case, there is room for a good deal of experiment on the attrition of shingle; that which has been done on flint pebbles does not suggest that they are very long-lived. But unless we envisage an origin of this sort we are no better off since, except in specific localities, it is difficult to assume that existing shingle beaches are solely the product of present-day wear and tear of cliffs. Zenkovich (p. 474) notes that: 'The Arabat spit is composed of shells, the gravel and shingle barriers on the east of the Chukchi Sea contain a diversity of rocks, among which those of igneous origin are plentiful, although the few headlands in the area are shales. On the basis of this and other attributes Kaplin has established that barrier material has been derived from the erosion of fluvio-glacial deposits of the sea floor.' Does this mean under present conditions, or that the material has gradually accumulated during a rise in sea-level? The problem remains effectively unsolved. The fact that shingle does move in localities where there are unusually strong tidal currents in no way contributes to the solution of our immediate problem.

In this little book any detailed discussion of waves and wave action is out of the question. Wind blowing over the sea produces waves which travel inwards long after the generating force has ceased. In an open ocean, with strong winds, waves may reach a height of about 50+feet. In more restricted seas the height is less. Local winds may set up waves which affect a particular stretch of coast; on the other hand, swell waves, the product of a distant storm, may roll in on any coast facing relatively open water. The wave pattern near the coast is naturally affected by the offshore configuration, and if the coast shelves gently, waves may break well seawards of the actual coastline. In whatever way the waves may have been formed, it is in broad terms possible to distinguish two main types as they affect the coast – constructive and destructive waves. These two terms were first used by W. V. Lewis.*

That some waves build up a beach, and that others destroy it, has been long known and observed. Lewis considered the subject more deeply, however, and pointed out that in destructive waves the main feature is the power of the backwash. These waves are usually steep and may be high. In breaking, the water plunges almost vertically downwards and may even curl seawards a trifle. In this way wave energy is expended and the swash may travel a relatively small distance up the beach. Constructive waves, on the other hand, break more regularly and less frequently, perhaps 5 to 8 a minute as compared with 10 to 20 a minute for destructive waves. Moreover, the breaking wave plunges far less vertically, and much more of the energy of the wave is transmitted to the swash which travels farther up the beach. A consequence of this is that since it has spread over a bigger area than the rather lifeless swash of a destructive wave, much more of it percolates into the beach, and so the ensuing backwash is minimised for that reason, and also by friction. The vertical plunge of a destructive wave is partly, even mainly, induced by the mass of water carried beachwards by its predecessor. This in turn implies a much more effective backwash, because the far greater volume of water on the beach means a less effective loss as a result of friction and percolation.

If constructive waves are breaking on a shingle beach during the rise from neap- to spring-tide level, they characteristically build a ridge which is driven up the beach. A similar effect may take place on a sand beach, where it is commonly called a berm, but it does not resemble the ridge on a shingle beach.

* *Geogrl J.*, **78**, 1931, 131.

King* notes that the 'chief characteristic of a berm is the marked break of slope at the seaward edge of a nearly horizontal platform; the height of the break of slope is usually a little above the mean high-water mark'. If the reader walks along any well-defined shingle ridge, he will usually see one or more minor ridges running parallel to its length on the seaward face. If, however, he revisits it after a severe storm, these will have disappeared and a new minor ridge will not form until later constructive waves act upon it. On a sandy beach destructive waves will destroy any berms which they cover, and will make a continuous, concave slope.

Barrier beaches (offshore bars) are beaches built by wave action in front of the actual shoreline. They may be of shingle or sand, or a mixture of the two. Shingle barriers are, in fact, rare. Because of the difficulty of moving pebbles and stones shoreward from deeper water, shingle barriers seem to be fed and maintained almost entirely by longshore movement. One of the best known is the Chesil Beach (p. 30). Scolt Head Island is a barrier beach, but there the amount of shingle is relatively small. Nearly all the major barrier beaches and islands are built of sand, and they are numerous. They are found all along the east coast of the United States south of New Jersey; there are many long and well-developed examples in the Gulf of Mexico; the nehrungen of the Baltic are of this type; the long sand beaches, including the 90-mile beach in Australia and numerous examples in West Africa, as well as the so-called Chenier plains between the Orinoco and the Amazon, belong to this type. There are also numerous examples around the coasts of Asia. Between them and the original coast there is either a shallow open lagoon, or strips of marsh and swamp. The barriers may be built up higher by wind-blown sand once the waves have raised them to about high-water level. This follows from the fact that they are characteristic of low sandy coasts, and that extensive flats, if in tidal seas, are exposed in front of them at low water. Shells or shingle, if present, are washed up to the top of the beach. The location of a barrier is determined mainly by the fact that the

* C. A. M. King, *Beaches and Coasts*, 1959, p. 248.

waves once broke along the *original* line of its formation, since the gradient of the shore was so gentle that the normal waves could not reach the inner coast.

Once parts of such a barrier rose above the level of normal waves and tides, seeds of plants carried to it by currents or in other ways would begin to take root, and grasses and various creepers soon spread. These, in their turn, form obstacles to wind-blown sand which sooner or later would begin to ac- cumulate around them. In this way small, individual dunes would form, join together, and eventually make a continuous dune ridge. In storms the ridge might be wholly or partly destroyed, but growth would begin once again. A time might eventually come when normal storms could no longer over- wash the ridge and dune system. But this does not mean that the feature has necessarily attained complete stability. The wind is likely to blow the dune sand inland so that, in fact, the dunes themselves are slowly moving inwards, and together with this movement the waves may also drive the beach land- wards. In this way the whole structure may gradually pass into and even across the lagoon and finally become attached to the mainland. This is a process that will certainly be helped if the particular coast on which the barrier is situated is sinking; conversely, on a rising coast the barrier is likely to widen sea- wards. Since vertical movements are usually very slow, how- ever, the possibilities of movements of this kind can be deduced only from the general physiography of the features involved (see p. 85).

Nowadays a beach is not only regarded as a most attractive natural feature; in many places of our own and other countries it is also an asset of considerable economic importance. This alone is sufficient to cause a local authority to take great trouble in its preservation. On the other hand, the movement of material along a coast may often have profound effects, often deleterious, on harbour and other installations. Hence the more we know about the lateral and other movement of beach material, the better.

A few years ago this knowledge had to be gained by general observation or by watching the movement of a few marked pebbles. It is true that conclusions obtained in this way were often valuable, but they were in no real sense quantitative; and were always empirical. Today there are various ways of obtaining far more accurate results. The usual methods employed are by noting movements of specially painted pebbles. It is now possible to paint stones with a paint that remains on them for a considerable time. A far better method, which has to be used with much discretion on account of health hazards, is to 'mark' the pebbles by some radioactive isotope. The marked material, pebbles, sand, or even mud, can be then put on the beach, dumped offshore or in an estuary, and its subsequent movements traced by means of a geiger counter. This means that the counter must be dragged over all the relevant parts of the sea or estuary floor and the work can be both tedious and expensive. Nevertheless, it gives good results. In an estuary the movement is either up- or down-stream, and so the problem is simpler; in the open sea marked stones or sand may move in any direction from the original place of deposition, so that a big area may have to be swept. Since the counter is unlikely to 'pick up' stones more than perhaps a foot away from it, or even but slightly buried by other stones or sand, it is clearly a difficult and delicate process to obtain detailed results even on a beach. Nevertheless, a number of most useful observations have been made. The other method is to use what are called fluorescent tracers: the sand or shingle used in the experiment is coated with a substance containing a fluorescent dye. Once it is dumped on the beach or that part of the sea floor *exposed at low water*, it can easily be traced at night by the light of an ultra-violet lamp. The coated grains are conspicuous, and since it is easily possible to use differently coloured grains, an experiment can be of a complex nature and not just confined to one set of marked stones or sand. Moreover, it also lends itself to more exact quantitative methods. If we know the general drift of material, samples of sand so marked can be put down at selected points, and their movements traced. The concentration measured is proportional to the rate of movement. A high concentration at any one point down-stream from the point of origin indicates a slow flow, whereas a low con-

centration implies a more rapid flow. It is a method more
easily used with shingle than sand.

A modification of this method, but less satisfactory, is to use
a range of different materials. These may or may not be of the
same specific gravity as the beach material, and lighter grains
will move greater distances than heavy ones. Often Nature
herself demonstrates this method. The erosion of a cliff of
some distinctive rock will clearly indicate the direction of
drift, but heavy materials are likely to be left behind. A somewhat similar effect is visible in Durham: coal sand and dust
dumped on the shore all too clearly indicates the direction of
drift!

The practice of aqualung diving has also been of no small
value in this context. Marked pebbles put down at surveyed
places off Scolt Head Island on the coast of Norfolk were
investigated in this way, and surprisingly little or even no
movement was recorded except in one or two instances. The
observations continued for some weeks, and further dives were
made about a year later. There is no doubt that this method
could be extended; and the recent work on submerged archeo-
logical sites in the Mediterranean and elsewhere has shown
how adaptable it is. Some geological survey work has also been
done by this method. A great deal depends on the clarity of the
water, and also on its temperature; depth, too, must be carefully considered. In general, warm seas lend themselves best to
this work but some excellent results have been obtained
around the coasts of Great Britain.

# 3. Accumulation and Accretion: Sand Dunes and Salt Marshes

In Chapter 2 it was shown how material moved along the coast, and how these movements could be observed and measured. We must now turn to a discussion of the accumulations to which they give rise. It will be apparent that they are likely to be more pronounced on a gently shelving bottom than on a steep one. It is well to re-emphasise that if there is a considerable tidal range, the waves and tidal currents acting upon the top of the beach when the tide is high may have a very different effect from wave action at low water. Moreover, at high water larger waves can approach the coast more easily. But if the bottom shelves very gently, the larger waves may break some distance from the beach. The waves exercise a sorting effect, and the coarser material, the shingle, is usually swept to the top of the beach, and so may be locally untouched at neap tides. Since, too, the tidal currents (p. 15) may run in contrary directions at different stages of the tide, it follows that there may be, for this reason, opposed movements of sand and other material on the upper and lower parts of the same beach.

The simplest form produced by lateral movement of beach material along a coast is the spit of sand which often forms across a river mouth or other inlet. The unattached end usually bends inwards, and at first the whole formation may be below sea-level. But sooner or later it builds up to form an extension of the adjacent beach. How far it will extend depends on local conditions including the supply of material, the configuration of the coast, and the strength of forces (waves, etc.) from directions opposed to the direction of growth. It is probable that, even if the beach from which it springs is shingly, the shingle will not spread along the spit until it has been built up above water-level. Sometimes spits of this sort show several former ends pointing landwards. These imply alternating periods of longitudinal and inward growth; the recurved ends as a rule indicate the work of waves; those from any seaward direction are likely to turn the free end of the spit inwards.

If there is an abundance of shingle, the recurved ends, or laterals, are likely to be prominent. Hurst Castle spit at the mouth of the Solent illustrates this very well. Sometimes spits grow outwards from either side of an inlet. Those enclosing Poole Harbour illustrate this action. What is unusual and so far unexplained about these two spits is that the northern one, the Sandbanks peninsula, is much narrower than the southern one.

Spits may, however, develop on a much larger scale. The southerly drift of shingle southwards along the coast of East Anglia has been responsible for the great spit which deflects the River Alde for about 11 miles. Whilst it is probably correct to say that this great accumulation is the product of southerly drifting, it is impossible to suppose that it is fed only from Norfolk and Suffolk. The amount of shingle that the cliffs of these two counties could produce would be entirely inadequate. In the past, before the coast to the north was cut back by erosion to its present position, there may have been more shingle. But one cannot help thinking that much of the Orford shingle must have come from the glacial deposits on the sea floor (see p. 21). Whatever the origin, a spit began to form near what is now the town of Aldeburgh, and it continued to grow southwards. Today there is a single wide ridge of shingle from Aldeburgh to near the lighthouse, where there are numerous recurved ridges, partly arranged in groups. Study of these ridges shows that some are cut across by newer ones, so that by careful mapping it is possible to trace the evolution of the spit (Fig. 5).

A little south of the lighthouse a number of ridges, pointing southwards, end abruptly near a place called Stonyditch Point. This implies that for a considerable time the southern

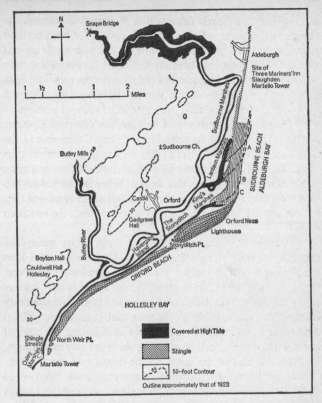

Fig. 5. *Orford Ness. The lines between A B C and the present coast (dotted) indicate the probable former outlines of the shingle spit.*

end of the whole formation was in this position. If we consider this place in relation to the position of the little town and castle of Orford we shall note that when the spit ended in this position Orford was in a favourable position for a mediaeval port. The castle was built in 1164–65, and then the town was at the height of its prosperity. May we not reasonably conclude that the period coincided with the many ridges ending at Stonyditch Point? Then, for some reason, the spit began to lengthen again, and as it did so Orford became increasingly difficult for ships to reach. Today it is impossible except for small craft at favourable times to enter the haven. If we examine, most easily on aerial photographs, the far end of the spit we shall see that it has on more than one occasion been cut short, and then lengthened. It may well have reached its maximum length just prior to the great storm of 1897. The waste of Orford's shingle accumulates on the other side of the haven at a place appropriately called Shingle Street.*

The coast of England and Wales affords many other major features of this sort. In the south-east the great shingle foreland of Dungeness has grown out into the Channel. The south and west facing side is still subject to erosion and shingle is swept round the point and accumulates on the up-Channel side. Its evolution is more complicated than that of Orford Ness. It is easily possible to trace the trend of the numerous ridges, but it is far less easy to account for the shingle travelling to the ness across Rye Bay. It has been pointed out that some *groups* of ridges are distinctly lower, or higher, than their neighbours. This has been taken to mean change of sea-level; and if that is so, it points to a very considerable age for the whole structure. Moreover, Dungeness is but the seaward end of a vast flat, most of which is called Romney Marsh. There are many problems still unsolved about the whole area, and a careful correlation of studies on the shingle and on the marsh, by bores and radio-carbon dating of deposits, is necessary before we can begin to understand the whole. The growth of the foreland has had marked effects on the Rother and other rivers draining the area (Fig. 6).

A quick survey round the coast of Britain will show many other deflections, usually on a smaller scale. Some of the best-known are the Yare at Great Yarmouth, the Exe and the Teign in Devon, the Alt in Lancashire, and the curious courses of the some of the streams in west Cumberland. This brief list omits many other well-known features such as the Chesil

* For an interesting account of the evolution of this part of the coast in Quaternary times, see A. P. Carr and R. E. Baker, *Trans. Inst. Br. Geogr.*, No. 45, 1968.

Beach, about 18 miles long, and showing from north-west to south-east an almost perfect grading of pebbles, and also a corresponding increase in height and breadth. It omits, too, the sand and shingle forelands in Cardigan Bay, of which Ro Wen, at the mouth of the Mawddach, Morfa Dyffryn, and

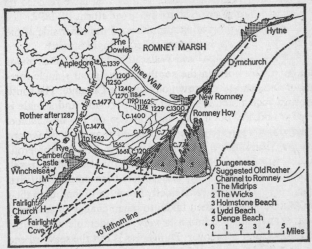

Fig. 6 *Dungeness and Romney Marsh. The broken lines indicate W. V. Lewis's view on the evolution of the shingle ridges. The dates give the times of inning of tracts of marsh.*

Morfa Harlech are the most important. These Welsh examples illustrate very well a point made by W. V. Lewis, namely that the main beaches of Cardigan Bay and other areas, turn, as far as local conditions allow, so that they run parallel to the main waves acting upon them. The increasing depth of the sea floor, however, prevents a full realisation of this process.

On the Norfolk coast there are many features of interest, and more detail will be given later in this chapter. The point to be made at this stage is that the two main features, Scolt Head Island and Blakeney Point, although superficially similar, are in fact very different. The former is strictly a barrier beach; it is not joined to the land. The latter is a spit in the sense that

the shingle ridge, which is its main feature, is continuous from
the Far Point to the glacial cliffs at Weybourne and Sheringham. Since the western part of Blakeney faces much shallower
water than the eastern end, it is at least possible that a spit
growing westwards from the cliffs united with what was once a
barrier beach. There is, however, nothing in the form and
nature of the beach to prove this.

Barrier beaches in other parts of the world often attain
great length. Those in the western part of the Gulf of Mexico
are almost entirely formed of sand built up by wave action,
and dunes have formed on their inner side. They are often
continuous for many miles; Padre Island is *c*. 130 miles long.
Zenkovich calls attention to a barrier, with some gaps, which
runs for almost 600 km along the coast of western Kamchatka;
in the Black Sea the Tendra spit is 92 km long, and in the
Caspian the Agrakan spit reaches 70 km.

Coastal barriers may begin as spits, or they may be built
up offshore and are then gradually pushed in to the coast.
Their general shape is the work of waves, and at low water
some of the sand dries and is blown inwards and sooner or
later begins to form dunes on the barrier. Barriers are extremely well developed in some parts of Australia. Fig. 7
shows the general nature of those enclosing the Gippsland
Lakes in south-eastern Victoria. The pattern of the ridges can
here too be used as a criterion of origin. If traces of former
recurves are visible, then it is argued that the formation started
its evolution as a spit. If, however, all the ridges are parallel to
the present shoreline, there is a much greater probability that
they originated offshore. In Fig. 7 both types are present. The
inner barrier grew first as a spit and later widened as a result
of accretion; the outer barrier began as a chain of offshore
islands which were lengthened by beach-drifting and later
joined together. The long barrier enclosing the Coorong in
South Australia is probably of similar origin. In Australia,
Bird argues that barriers are best developed where there is a
dominant ocean swell, and a smallish tidal range. If the range
is large, it helps to develop and maintain gaps in the barrier.
The outer barriers are usually lower than the inner ones.

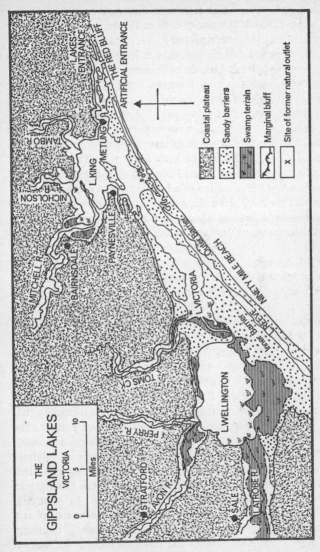

Fig. 7. *The Gippsland Lakes, Victoria. (After E. C. F. Bird.)*

THE
GIPPSLAND
LAKES

VICTORIA

Miles
0    5    10

Coastal plateau
Sandy barriers
Swamp terrain
Marginal bluff
x   Site of former natural outlet

LAKES ENTRANCE
THE RED BLUFF
ARTIFICIAL ENTRANCE
TAMBO R.
NICHOLSON R.
L. KING
METUNG
MITCHELL R.
BAIRNSDALE
PAYNESVILLE
L. VICTORIA
Outer Barrier
NINETY MILE BEACH
REEVE
L. VICTORIA
Inner Barrier
TOMS CK.
PERRY R.
STRATFORD
AVON R.
L. WELLINGTON
SALE
LATROBE R.

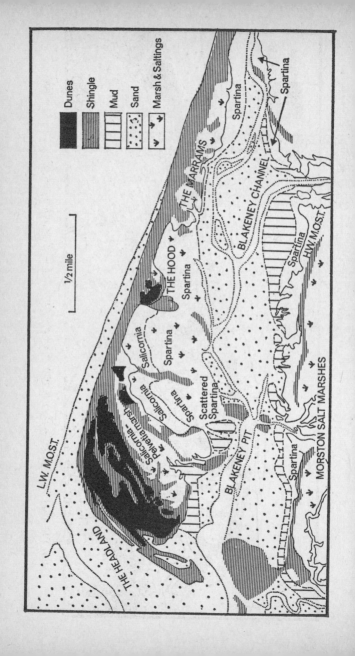

LW. M.O.S.T.

THE HEADLAND

Pewtla marsh

Salicornia

Salicornia

Salicornia

Spartina

Spartina

Scattered Spartina

Spartina

THE HOOD

Spartina

THE MARRAMS

Spartina

Spartina

BLAKENEY CHANNEL

Spartina

H.W. M.O.S.T.

BLAKENEY PIT

Spartina

MORSTON SALT MARSHES

½ mile

Dunes
Shingle
Mud
Sand
Marsh & Saltings

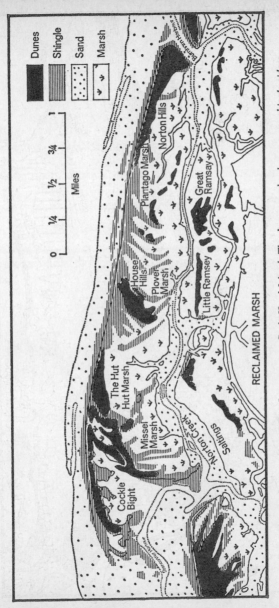

Fig. 8. Top map: *Blakeney Point*. Lower map: *Scolt Head Island. The dunes nearly always cover shingle ridges.*

Many parts of the west African coast, e.g. near Lagos, show old barrier formations very well.

The two best examples in Britain, although barriers in one sense, have evolved rather as spits. Scolt Head Island, in Norfolk, shows by the numerous recurves that it has grown from east to west, but nevertheless there is no reason for thinking that the older eastern part has moved westwards. On the Moray Firth coast, near Nairn, there is a most interesting feature, the Bar, at first sight very similar to Scolt. But observation from year to year shows that shingle removed from its eastern, and particularly its mid part, is carried along it by beach-drifting and accumulates as a fine series of recurves at its south-western end. Study of old maps also shows that the whole feature has moved considerably to the south-west in the last two or three centuries, and this movement is still continuing.

The fullest analysis of the movement of material alongshore has been made by Zenkovich, and readers desiring more detailed knowledge are referred to his book. He speaks of sand and/or shingle flow and gives many instances of types of accumulation. It is of interest to quote (pp. 409–410):

'Two ports have been constructed 80 km apart on the Caucasian Black Sea coast at Gagra (1914) and Sochi (1937–8). Both cut across shingle flows of approximately 20 000 m³ and 30 000 m³ per annum. During construction of the port of Gagra the shingle beach in front of the jetty facing the flow began to move so rapidly that it became clear that it would be impossible to protect the port from shallowing (Bozhich, 1930, 1938). When the jetty had reached a distance of 200 m from the shore, construction was discontinued.

'The same phenomena occurred at Sochi (Gamazhenko, 1947, 1950; Zenkovich, 1947d, 1948a), but despite the great volume of the flow the increase in the shingle beach has been far slower and the port has now been in operation for twenty years without any threat of the accumulation of shingle reaching its mouth.

'When an explanation was sought, it was found that the

direction of the coast relative to the wave resultant differed. At Sochi the angle was not more than 4–6° (Zhdanov, 1950), whereas at Gagra the angle was 20°. Because of this the length of beach on which accretion occurred was more than 5 km at Sochi, but less than 1 km at Gagra. It also explains why the flow with the smaller volume built up the coast at the port of Gagra far more rapidly (Zenkovich, 1948a). Sochi might possibly be adversely affected at some time in the future by the accumulation of shingle, but at present the shingle is being removed for building purposes.'

The same phenomena can be seen in numerous places around our own coasts, noticeably in eastern and southern England. Great Yarmouth harbour piers cause an accumulation on their north side (Yarmouth denes); Gorleston and the coast to the south have suffered severe erosion, but now there are extensive sea defences. The same is true on a smaller scale north and south both of Lowestoft and Southwold, and on the south coast west and east of Shoreham and other places. But let it not be thought that it is all as simple as this. There is serious erosion, now held by a sea wall, on the Norfolk coast between Happisburgh and Sea Palling. A little farther south and east at Winterton Ness there is an area of accretion. The erosion at Dunwich is referred to on page 81, but two or three miles farther south the cliffs at Sizewell are now inside ridges on which dunes have formed. Precise reasons for these sudden changes are not known; the possible reasons for them may be surmised, but a full explanation is not forthcoming.

This leads to another matter of practical importance. There is now a great demand for sand and shingle, and coastal deposits are very tempting to potential users. It is by no means easy to give a simple answer to anyone who asks if material can be moved from a certain place either on- or offshore without causing any adverse effect upon the coast. This matter needs consideration under at least two heads – the conservation of features of scientific interest and the possibility of provoking erosion. The fully reported discussion of the enquiry on the building of a power station at Dungeness showed only too clearly the divergence between what may be called the economic and the conservationist points of view.

Shingle forelands like Dungeness are valuable areas of study of the formation and evolution of shingle ridges. The part near the point, including that occupied by the new power station, is significant. It is the part of the area which suffers erosion – the station has already had to be protected – and its loss leads to the growth of new ridges on the other side of the point. Moreover, the whole of the shingle forms a unit. From air photographs it is easy to map all the ridges, and they can be levelled on the ground, so that the evolution of the foreland can be understood. The building of the station has destroyed many ridges, and any extension will destroy more. Removal of shingle for other purposes has the same effect. In other words, Dungeness in its natural state was our largest and most complex shingle formation, and was of high scientific interest and importance; parts of Orford Ness still remain untouched. Bombing has pitted many ridges, but not seriously disturbed them. Unfortunately, the interesting part near the lighthouse is nowadays unapproachable on account of Ministry of Defence installations. In one sense some installations may have a 'preservative' effect, but their actual effects must be uncertain. The building of a power station at any part of the coast is likely to have some deleterious results. These must be recognised and, of course, met. But while everyone must recognise the necessity for them, it should also be essential that agreement between what might broadly be called the economic and conservation points of view is obtained for all, or at least for long stretches of the coast *before* lengthy and expensive enquiries are held about any one site.

The removal of material from the sea floor near the coast may be dangerous; removal probably means deepening of the water, and therefore increased wave action, and consequently increased erosion. It is at least vitally important to know that material is moving laterally into the place from which it is removed. The removal of material offshore from Hall Sands in south Devon is held, with good reason, to have been the cause of serious erosion there. We have to learn much more about this kind of problem before we can speak with authority. The converse of this problem occurs sometimes in dredging. Sediments dredged from the Mersey and the Thames were deposited well out to sea, but it was noticed that sooner or later they found their own way back. Similarly, the removal of sand or shingle from a beach may cause first a lowering, and then increased erosion, and possibly also a decreased sand supply for the dunes. The important point is that each and every locality needs careful investigation before permission is given for removal of material from the beach or offshore (see Chapter 7).

It is now practicable, by means of carefully devised scale models of a locality, to find out by experiment what is likely to be the result of the removal of sand, shingle, or mud. We shall have occasion elsewhere to refer to the work of the Hydraulics Research Station, but a visit to the station or a glance through its annual reports should be enough to convince local authorities and others concerned that a demand, however tempting economically, to remove material in any quantity should in most cases certainly be granted only in the light of careful experiment. It is true that local people may be right in their views that no damage may follow removal, but in this present age, once the use of powerful dredgers and other machinery is put into effect, it is too late to reverse the process. The economic pressures for the removal may only too easily overcome the opinions of local experts if those opinions cannot be backed by facts.

Accumulations take many forms, and once a feature has been built it undergoes a continuous evolution. A feature may be fed by new material on only one side or on both sides; and the rate of supply to each side may be very different. Fig. 9 gives in somewhat simplified form some of the more common ways in which sand and/or shingle can accumulate. Some forms are attached to the original coast, others are free. Sometimes a small island is joined to the shore by what is usually called a tombolo. The same process is sometimes seen if a wreck is driven ashore, but still remains some distance from the beach. The waves playing round it build a tail which

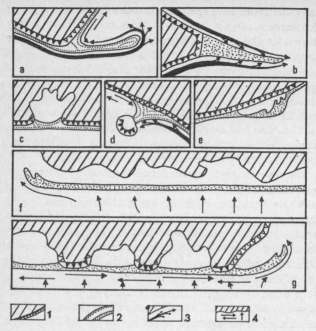

Fig. 9. *Accumulation forms:* a, *spit;* b, *tongue (accretes on both sides);* c, *barrier beach;* d, *tombolo;* e, *looped spit;* f, *beach barrier;* g, *beach barrier attached to parts of the original coast.*

1 = *mainland and active cliff;* 2 = *dead cliff and coast with beach;* 3 = *flow of material and its supply to the coast and out to sea;* 4 = *migration of material along the edge of an accumulation form and supply of material from the bottom.*

*(After V. P. Zenkovich:* Processes of Coastal Development. *First English edition published by Oliver & Boyd, 1967.)*

sooner or later joins it to the beach, although not all of it need be above water. Loops of sand and shingle are often formed behind small islands, and small bars may join islands or reefs together. A visit to the Isles of Scilly will show several of these features. The disintegration of the granite gives rise to sandy beaches, often somewhat coarse, and small tombolos and other forms have been built between islands and adjacent skerries or rocks, e.g. between St Agnes and Gugh. In Orkney there is an abundance of interesting coastal forms. The most common are the ayres and oyces. Ayres are primarily shingle bars built as bars across the mouths of small bays; the oyces are the sheets of water impounded by them. One or two islands, e.g. Stronsay, Shapinsay are in fact a number of smaller islets joined together by this process. In Shetland, too, shingle bars in bays and inlets are not uncommon. Island groups, where the water between islands is fairly shallow, are ideal localities for the growth of this type of shore feature.

The ways in which accumulation forms affect the appearance of the coast depend much on the nature of the coast on which they have formed. In England and Wales there is a wide difference in appearance between Scolt Head Island, an unattached barrier, and the ridge enclosing Slapton Ley on the south Devon coast. On the south coast of the Lleyn peninsula (Caernarvonshire) the shingle ridges in the bays on either side of Pwllheli are interesting. They run approximately eastwards to join the former small islands of Careg-yr-Imbill and Pen-ychan to the mainland. Moreover, they illustrate very well the relation of beach structure to the size of waves. The eastern end of these two beaches, and of one or two others on this coast, are higher and more massive and built of much larger pebbles than the western ends. The small islands act as great groynes and the prevalent south-westerly winds and waves cause a drifting of material to the eastern ends of the beaches. The western ends are much lower, and even sandy. The beaches impound areas of alluvium and so are comparable in this respect with Slapton Ley.

Some of the more interesting beaches in Britain occur in the Outer Hebrides. Not only are they interesting because of the way in which the various beaches form small barriers and spits, but, also in some of the islands, on account of the nature of the sand which forms them. The blown sand, almost completely calcareous, behind the beaches is known as the machair. It is derived from the beaches; it forms dunes at the head of the beach but more characteristically a low sandy plain behind them. The sea shallows very gradually off South Uist, Tiree and some other islands. The beaches are wide, and in South Uist long, extending between two rocky headlands. Usually the beaches are topped by a shingle ridge inside of which are some low dunes. The sand is entirely shell sand and gives a very fertile sward. It receives humus in various ways; large numbers of barnacle geese visit it in winter, the sea casts up an abundance of seaweed, especially Laminaria, and there is also a supply of animal dung. Seaweed is also spread over the machair by the crofters.

The strong westerly winds and the not infrequent gales play a large part in the formation of the machair, the sand of which spreads as a layer, rather than accumulating as dunes. The surface, often interrupted by lochs, needs constant attention otherwise it is all too easily destroyed by erosion. Seen on a bright summer's day the machair is remarkably beautiful. There are numerous wild flowers, which provide both scent and colour; the green of the sward, the brilliant white of the beaches, the mountains behind in South Uist and Barra, and the blue ocean to the west make an unforgettable picture. Here, as elsewhere, the marram grass (*Psamma arenaria*) is the main accretor of dunes, and if for some reason this is destroyed, severe damage may accrue to the machair within.

In Harris and Lewis machair, in the way in which it is found in South Uist, is somewhat rare, but there are several wide areas of blown sand and dunes on the west coast. The sand formations in Traigh Luskentyre are extensive. Many of the small islands between the bigger ones are largely or wholly composed of sand, and some are known to have changed shape in the course of time, since sand is carried from one part to another. The small island of Vallay is particularly interesting. A submerged forest is visible at low springs on its western coast, and it was noted in 1794 that some land had disappeared within living memory, and occasionally when a dune was blown away, remains of earlier houses were exposed.

SAND DUNES

In some parts of Britain it is possible, as we have seen, to distinguish shingle from sand formations. Orford Ness is entirely formed of shingle, so too is the Chesil Beach. Shingle also builds all of Dungeness proper; there is blown sand near Camber, an area quite distinct from the shingle foreland. The major beach at Blakeney is almost entirely shingle. Other places such as the forelands in Cardigan Bay, especially Morfa Harlech and Morfa Dyffryn, the Bar at Nairn and the Culbin Sands, the sands of Forvie and the bar (the Warren) at the mouth of the Exe are examples of both sand and shingle formations. In these the shingle is nearly always the skeleton on which sand dunes have formed. Elsewhere, but more commonly outside Britain, there are major sand bars, like those in the Gulf of Mexico and along nearly all the eastern coast of the United States south of New York, in which shingle plays no part, or at the most a very subsidiary one. Because of this close interrelation of sand and shingle, and even more because of the great amount of sand available, it will be convenient to say something of the formation of coastal sand dunes at this stage.

Dune sands around the coast are nearly always the direct result of wind blowing over sandy beaches and flats exposed and partly dried at low water. Anyone walking along such a beach on a windy day is made fully aware of the large amounts of sand that are moved. The direction of movement may be along the beach, landwards, or seawards. That which is moved seawards is more than likely to be returned to the beach by wave action at a later time. That which is moved along the beach may help in its lengthening, especially if the beach continues as a spit across a bay or re-entrant. That which is carried inland is likely to form dunes but (see below) may help to fill lagoons and modify the surface of mud flats.

Once the waves have built up a beach, whether of sand or shingle, so that its top is awash only in exceptional storms or tides, the possibility of dune formation is present. Any obstacle on the beach, some driftwood, a large boulder, or the shingle ridge itself if there is one, forms a barrier to the sand carried by the wind, and will bring about some deposition. In its early stages deposition will form a low hillock which, if the obstacle is a solid one, will gather on its windward side. It may be continued downwind as two arms on either side of the obstacle. Sooner or later the heap itself becomes the obstacle, but its upward growth may be spasmodic or irregular because under some conditions sand may be removed from it. If sand blows on to a shingle ridge a good deal will penetrate between the pebbles, but most is likely to form a crest to the ridge, but here too deposition is favoured around obstacles of one sort or another.

The factor of vegetation must now be introduced. Anyone who knows sandy beaches is equally familiar with the common sand dune grass, marram, which, although of overwhelming importance, is not necessarily the pioneer in dune formation. This lot is usually fulfilled in England by *Agropyrum junceiforme*, a grass that, at first sight, resembles marram, but is less rigid, somewhat darker in colour, and has an entirely different flowering spike. It can grow at slightly lower levels than marram, and can put up with a certain amount of wave action and tidal inundation. However, both grasses spread in much the same way. Seeds, carried by wind or other agents, are dropped on the sand or shingle ridge, and if circumstances are suitable, take root and send up a shoot. The *Agropyrum* will be commoner at lower levels. Once, however, some blades appear above the surface they become obstacles, and deposition will begin to take place around them. Once these small tumps of sand are safe from any but exceptional wave action, marram replaces *Agropyrum*. Marram thrives best where there is a good sand supply. The grass grows upward with the accreting sand. Each tump behaves similarly, and sooner or later neighbouring ones unite and embryo dunes form. If they are on a new ridge crest, a time will soon come, provided that there is an adequate sand supply, when they unite together to form at first a rather irregular, but more or less continuous dune ridge. As the whole ridge grows, it becomes an even greater obstacle and it soon becomes a typical fore dune. Its future depends largely on what happens in front of it. On a shallow foreshore it is common for the waves to throw up a new ridge in front of the old one, once shallowing has reached a sufficient degree. Or, if the original ridge were one of a recurved series, it is more than likely that it will be succeeded by a newer recurve. Whatever the circumstances, once the newer ridge has formed, it will become the obstacle. New dunes will begin to form on it, and the supply of sand to the older ridge will be cut off, or partly cut off. In this way several low dune ridges may form, and in Britain they are seen to advantage in places like the western ends of Blakeney Point and Scolt Head Island, on the sandy forelands of Cardigan Bay, and elsewhere where there is a wide sand beach.

If, however, a new ridge does not form in front of the original one, the dunes may continue to grow both in height and area. It is difficult to say what really determines the height of a dune. In England and Wales they seldom exceed 60 ft. Higher ones nearly always stand on some solid high ground. In the Culbin Sands, under natural conditions, they reached about 100 ft. In Australia many dunes have migrated on to rocky knobs and promontories to reach notably high levels. Bird states that the dunes on Stradbroke Island, in southern Queensland, reach more than 900 ft from sea-level.

Almost all sand dunes are in a constant state of change, partly for the reasons already given and partly because the wind seldom ceases to have some effect on them. If a dune ridge grows up unhindered by another in front of it, it will also probably move inland. Sand blown up the windward side carries over the crest to fall down the lee side. This process is checked, perhaps for some time halted, by vegetation, but inward moving dunes are very common. If the winds are variable the rate and direction of movement will be less regular, and the dune pattern may be complex. On a sea beach where dunes have formed along the coast, the waves in storms and surges will erode the dune foot, and where the dunes are low may completely overwash them. Erosion implies that bare sand is exposed, some of which may be blown inland.

A special form of dune, called a parabolic dune, is characteristic of sea coasts. In its simplest form its evolution may be

pictured as follows: suppose that there is a fore dune which is
growing in height; it is held by vegetation, and if we suppose
it is lower at its ends than in its mid part, these lower parts
may be anchored by vegetation. The higher middle part,
under the action of strong and persistent winds may continue
to advance, so that in course of time a somewhat crescent-
shaped dune is formed in which the hollow of the crescent
*faces* the wind. This is the opposite of what happens in
deserts; there a dune, originally formed around some obstacle continues to grow, but sand is more easily carried
round its flanks, and it is not long before the dune has two
horns pointing down wind, and the crescent enclosed between
them is in the lee of the dune, which is called a barkhan. The
difference between these two types is simply the result of
vegetation.

Another significant factor in the formation of dunes is the
sediment flow along the coast (see p. 16). Flows of this sort
may bring more and more sand to the beach, and so afford
ample supplies for dune growth. Zenkovich calls attention to an
extensive area of dunes on west Kamchatka which formed
near the southern end of such a flow. A similar occurrence is
found at Cape Peschanyy on the eastern side of the Caspian
Sea. The same author also emphasises the important distinction between the conditions under which dunes will form, and
the reasons for their formation. 'The conditions are the existence of a favourable wind regime and large reserves of sand in
the coastal zone. The reasons are the existence of a specific
supply of sand to a given locality and the rate of supply.'
(Zenkovich, p. 615.)

The appearance of dunes alters noticeably with age. Around
our own coasts, where much of the sand is siliceous, the dunes
at first are the same colour as the sand and are spoken of as
yellow dunes. It is at this stage that marram grass thrives at its
best. As time goes on, and assuming some stability, other
plants begin to invade the dunes, phanerogams, mosses and
lichens. Sooner or later these have an effect on the soil, and
gradually the yellow dunes give way to grey dunes. At this
stage the dunes are stable unless for some particular reason the

sand is caused to move. This can happen in all sorts of ways. Plants, even in the grey stage, seldom form a close turf, and it is always possible for the wind to begin blowing on a small expanse of bare sand and gradually to enlarge it. The same thing may happen, and did happen very often before myxomatosis depleted the rabbit population of our islands, as a result of rabbits burrowing in the dunes. People walking over the dunes and making paths expose the sand. Whatever the cause may be, once the bare sand is exposed the wind may well regain mastery, and so enlarge the hollow, and continue to do so until a large blow-out or even a complete cut through the dune ridge is made. The same process may also lead to the formation of parbolic dunes. It is because dunes are so easily destroyed that great care should always be taken in places where many people walk on the dunes, especially if that part of the coast is subject to erosion.

There are many fine coastal dunes in Britain. In England on the north coast of Cornwall the dunes east of St Ives, at Perranporth, Harlyn and Constantine bays, are extensive, and those at Braunton Burrows in north Devon have been the site of much ecological work. There are numerous areas of dunes on the Bristol Channel coast of Wales. In Cardigan Bay the dunes at Morfa Dyffryn still retain a wild appearance, and in winter the lows are temporarily converted into shallow lakes. On Morfa Harlech the dunes are advancing over the flats behind, and they are in one sense part of the same system as those at Morfa Bychan on the other side of the estuary. Tremadoc Bay is a unit in the sense that both waves and winds drive material to it along the coasts of Cardigan bay and the Lleyn peninsula. Farther north, between Mersey and Ribble, there are fine dunes, and again on the Cumberland coast. On the east coast those at Blakeney and Scolt Head Island show a clear relation to the shingle ridges. The narrow dune belt east and south of Happisburgh is at the present time protected by a sea wall built since the 1953 surge, but in its natural state it was somewhat unusual since it faced a fairly narrow beach, and formed a relatively thin line between the sea and the Broads. In Lincolnshire the dunes, once continuous all along the coast,

are now best developed in the south near Skegness and Gibraltar Point, and north of Mablethorpe. The part in between is
now almost a man-made coast, and has been heavily defended
since 1953, when the storm did severe damage. There are some
dunes at Spurn Head, and extensive developments along the
Northumberland coast. In fact, it may be said that almost
every bay or inlet around our coast possesses some sandhills,
however small they may be.

The same is true of many parts of Scotland, and in order to
illustrate the interest and variety of dune landscapes we shall
pay particular attention to the Culbin Sands and the Sands of
Forvie. The Culbin Sands lie between Nairn and Findhorn,
and the Bar (p. 36) is adjacent to them. The sands now are
largely afforested, and the expanse of bare sand is relatively
small. They rest on a raised flat on which there are numerous
shingle ridges, and the dunes have been blown up by the
westerly winds which carry the sand along the coast. The area
was first planted in 1839 and much of this woodland was cut
down in the First World War. Although sand had undoubtedly been blowing here for centuries, no great dunes seem to have
formed until the end of the seventeenth century. Before that
time the eastern end of the flats was in part a fertile farm and
carried the house of Culbin and a number of bothies. Farming
continued up to 1694, but by that date the sand from the west
was beginning to encroach on the fields, and it was decided
that it was useless to fight it any longer. Sand increased, the
fields and surrounding flats were covered, and eventually dunes
reaching 100 ft above sea-level grew up. The relatively sudden
change from a fertile farm to an arid waste was provocative of
many stories and legends all implying the sudden inundation
of the area by sand. This certainly was not the case. An Act of
Parliament, 1695, makes it certain that the sand had been
blowing for years, and it was not until the end of the seventeenth century that it became too big a problem to deal with it
any longer. We may assume that prior to this storms caused
serious difficulties every now and again, and if, as there is good
reason to believe, the estate was somewhat financially em-
barrassed at that time, it is easy to understand that evacuation

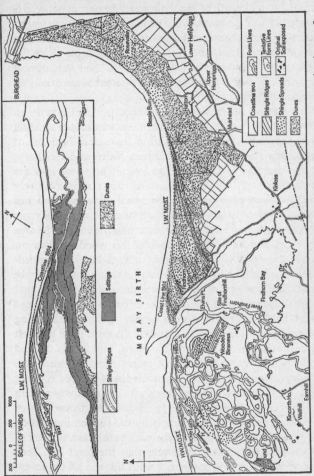

Fig. 10. *The Culbin Sands, Burghead Bay, and The Bar, 1937. The form lines represent the shapes of dunes at Culbin.*

finally became essential. The cottages were buried, but it is almost certain that although Culbin House also disappeared it was partly dismantled first. The remains of the house re-appeared once in the eighteenth century, and more stones were removed. Today it is not so easy to appreciate what this part of the coast looked like as it was before the 1939–45 war. Then there were several great dunes, the windward slopes of which were gentle, and their lee slopes steep, at the angle of rest of dry sand. In one or two places the movements of the sand had exposed the old plough land, and furrows and ridges were clearly seen. The high dunes were in the central part of the foreland; on the northern margin there were lower and newer ridges generally parallel with the shore. A little to the west of this main mass, at Maviston, there is a remarkably fine parabolic dune which has advanced over old woodland. This process still continues, and the advancing sand is burying trees, whereas on the inner side the stumps over which the sand has passed stand bare and gaunt. The changes at Culbin have been more spectacular than in most other places, but that such changes are not catastrophic is best shown by a comment made by Brigadier Bagnold: 'As a result of a calculation I made, I found that if a wind were to blow over this area [Culbin] for twenty-four hours at an average speed of 40 miles an hour and the sand which the wind carried on to the area was deposited over a depth downwind of one mile, then the great-est thickness of sand which could be deposited would be only one inch. Moreover, the wind at 40 miles an hour would have to blow against such high resistance due to the sand movement that it would be equivalent, upwind in an open country where there was not any sand, to a continuous wind of nearly 70 miles an hour.' (*Geogrl J.*, **90**, 1937, 498 (in Discussion).) Scientific analysis of this sort is the most effective means of killing the idea of a sudden inundation.

The sands of Forvie are at the mouth of the Ythan in Aberdeenshire. The area forms a peninsula, in the form of a spit, and there is an irregular dune ridge parallel to the sea, and another roughly coincident with the river margin. But the main masses of sand are near the southern end and form great parabolic dunes which trend across the peninsula and move northwards, and as they do so they also expand. There are now seven such waves. It is possible to correlate the movement with archaeological and historical evidence (Fig. 11). In the south of the area are some stone circles (B) probably of early Iron Age date, built on several feet of sand. It seems probable that the first sand wave reached or passed this site about 0 B.C. $\pm$ 100 years. At another site (C) a community lived from about A.D. 700–1400. This is supported by documentary evidence, and also by the remains of a small chapel. There is a legend, like that at Culbin, of a sudden overwhelming in 1413 which buried the village, but here, too, the process was undoubtedly far more gradual. Later maps and documents suggest that this first wave reached its present position in or about 1782. It was followed by other waves (see map), but it is thought that there has been little change in the last 200 years. Thus, as one traverses the sands from south to north, the waves are of increasing age and stability; the southernmost dune is still formed largely of bare sand. The intermediate dunes are all mobile with the exception of number 3 where, as on number 1, there is an almost complete cover of vegetation on windward and leeward sides, although there are local hollows of erosion. With this change there is also a change in the soil, an overall fall in pH and a rise in organic matter. Between the several waves there are plains, produced in part by deflation, cut down to the water-table. There are often small dune ridges with marram in these places.*

The correlation of dune movement with historical change is known in other places. Perhaps the most interesting changes

* The short account of the sands of Forvie is based on Dr S. Y. Landsberg's thesis, 'The Morphology and Vegetation of the Sands of Forvie' (Aberdeen, 1955). Since writing the manuscript of this book I have had occasion to revisit the sands and discuss their problems. I think it is unlikely that the sand waves have advanced in the way Dr Landsberg suggests. Each new wave would deprive its predecessor of an abundant sand supply, and it is difficult, in the scheme put forward by Dr Landsberg, to see why the waves should widen so much. Much more attention must be given to the glacial beds on which the higher parts of the sands rest; these, as she admits, could supply much sand. Moreover, southeasterly winds may well have played an important role. In brief, I think Dr Landsberg's scheme is too precise.

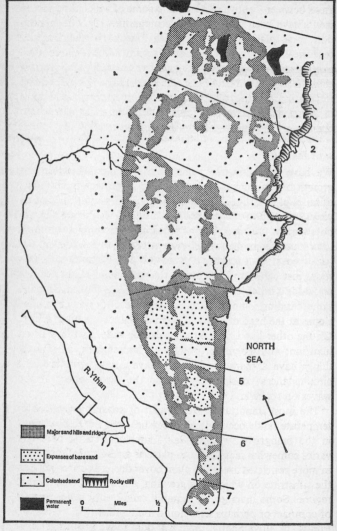

Fig. 11. *The Forvie Sands. (After S. Y. Landsberg in* The Vegetation of Scotland, *edited by J. H. Burnett. Oliver & Boyd, 1964.)*

have taken place in south Wales. There are many large dunes areas between Tenby and Cardiff in some of which sand movements have been of considerable magnitude. Serious inundation took place at Penard in the fourteenth and fifteenth centuries. The same is true at Margam Abbey, where sand overwhelmed buildings in about 1300, and at Kenfig. Similar changes took place on the Cornish coast, and it is interesting to note that the thirteenth and fourteenth centuries were times of great storminess. It is also at least possible that these changes were helped by slight movements of sea-level.

SALT MARSHES

We have just discussed some of the relations between the growth of sand dunes and vegetation. Along many hundreds of miles of coastline, vegetation of one sort or another plays a very important role. At low levels the algae (seaweeds) are noteworthy, but more from a botanical or ecological point of view than from that of physiography. Along much of the rocky coast of western Scotland the colour banding of the rocks just below and just above the water line is conspicuous, and adds a notable element to the scenery. In the sea lochs the same banding is noticeable, but because of the much gentler slopes at the head of many of them the bands are much wider. On the other hand, in the rather deeper water there are often luxuriant and extensive growths of laminarians, which certainly have a marked effect on wave action, and in some circumstances considerably reduce the direct effect of the waves on rocks and cliffs.

The most important development of coastal vegetation in temperate lands occurs in salt marshes, and in tropical areas in the mangrove swamps. Salt marsh vegetation naturally varies somewhat frcm place to place as a result of climate, but in more restricted areas the plant cover depends principally on the substrate on which it is growing, and also upon the tidal regime. Some marshes are notably sandy, others are formed of compact or perhaps semi-liquid mud and silt. In the Bay of Fundy, in Nova Scotia, there is a tidal range at springs of 40 ft; on many parts of our own coast a range of between 8 and

20 ft is common. On the other hand, in the Caribbean, where there is a solar tide, the extreme range is about 1 ft. These figures do not, of course, include the exceptional high waters of surges or hurricanes, but these phenomena, although they may cause serious erosion, or sweep masses of material from one place to another, have relatively little direct effect on the normal processes of sedimentation and plant growth.

Marsh growth usually takes place in sheltered localities, such as the estuaries of rivers, behind barrier islands or sandspits or along the inner parts of flat shelving coasts. The material of which they are formed is water-borne and consists of the finest particles of mineral matter derived, in the first place, by erosion. It would, however, be almost impossible in many, perhaps in most, cases to find its place of origin. If, as often happens, marsh growth takes place within sandy beaches, a great deal of sand may from time to time be blown over the marshes which will then show a rough stratification of fine and coarser material. Since the general principles of marsh growth are much the same everywhere, it will perhaps be simplest to describe what happens in a hypothetical case. Suppose that on a gently shelving sandy coast there is an offshore barrier island between which and the mainland there is a shallow channel or lagoon. The barrier island may be simple in outline; it may carry a number of recurved or lateral ridges (see p. 40) on its inner side. In either case, if the lagoon is tidal, and if the tidal range is considerable, part or even all of the lagoon may empty at low water. When the flood tide runs in it will, in the earlier stages, cover the sandy lagoon floor as a more or less uniform sheet of shallow water. Around the margins, in quiet places, and at the period when flood gives place to ebb and the water is, apart from any wind action, temporarily stagnant, deposition of mud and silt takes place. Perhaps the next tide, especially if helped by wind and waves, may remove much or all of the material thus deposited, but in course of time small banks of mud begin to form. If the inner edge of the barrier beach is divided into compartments by lateral ridges (recurves), deposition is likely to take place between them, especially if the entry to any such compartment is narrow so that the enclosed water is for the most part unaffected by any disturbance occurring in the main lagoon. The floor of this lagoon may be irregular and deposition may take place more readily on the higher, shallower places. As time goes on, all these small banks and patches of mud grow both in area and in height. Growth will be irregular and spasmodic; sometimes loss through erosion will destroy them in part, but over a long period of time growth, possibly irregular, is maintained.

As growth goes on, other changes take place. Both on the original sand flat and on the mud banks, seaweeds (algae) may begin to colonise, and once this has happened the algae themselves become trappers of silt and help to build up and to stabilise the mud banks. But algae do not thrive much above the level of low neap tides, and it is only a matter of time and local circumstances before the seeds of plants are carried to the banks and take root. The seeds are carried by the tides, some are blown by wind, others may be brought by birds or in some other way. However, some may find a lodgement in some favourable spot, possibly in a tangle of seaweed. The first plants to grow will be those tolerant of regular coverings by seawater, and those capable of growing on mud or sand. These plants only begin to grow when the processes of deposition have raised the banks above the levels covered permanently at low water, or, of course, in those places originally within the tidal range. In this country perhaps the commonest plant at this stage is the samphire (*Salicornia* spp.). This plant is found on firm mud or sand, but in wetter places, where the water does not drain easily away at low tide, eel or wigeon grass (*Zostera* spp.) is more common. On sandy areas the common salt marsh grass (*Puccinellia*, formerly *Glyceria*) is a pioneer. In many places the annual suaeda (*Suaeda maritima*) accompanies the *Salicornia*, and both may soon be invaded by the sea aster (*Aster tripolium*). When these stages are attained, the banks are likely to grow more quickly because the vegetation acts as a filter and causes more rapid deposition.

After this stage a variety of plants may colonise the marshes, and their nature will vary somewhat from place to place. On our east coast, where the marshes are usually (not always) built of firm mud, the sea pink (*Armeria maritima*), *Spergularia*, sea lavender (*Limonium humile*), and the sea arrow grass (*Triglochin maritimum*) are abundant, and characteristic of the middle levels. At the top of the marsh rushes, especially *Juncus maritimus* and *J. gerardii*, the sea-plantain (*Plantago coronopus*), and wormwood (*Artemisia maritima*) are common. In addition to these, there is another plant which is of great significance at middle levels. *Halimione portulacoides* (sea orache) characteristically begins its growth along the edges of creeks where drainage is good. It is a bushy, woody, lowlying plant with thick leafage so that it is a good accretor of silt. From the creek edges it spreads, often rapidly, over much of the marsh, and may obliterate other vegetation. On the south coast of England, the particular kind of rice or cord grass, known as *Spartina townsendii*, is the major component of most marshes. It is a natural hybrid and was first noticed in Southampton Water in 1870. Any reader familiar with that inlet and Poole Harbour will appreciate its effect on accretion. It is so useful in this way that it is often planted to collect silt and mud and to raise the level of certain places. In this way, and also by purely natural methods, it is now spreading far from its place of origin. Another characteristic of some of our south-coast marshes is that they are less compact, much softer and more water-logged than those of the east coast. On the other hand, the west-coast marshes, well developed in the estuaries and behind the sand and shingle forelands of Cardigan Bay, in the Dee estuary, and around Morecambe Bay are much more sandy. This is also true of some of the Scottish marshes, such as those behind the Bar off the Culbin Sands (p. 36).

Marshes will continue to grow in height naturally as long as they are covered by tidal water. It follows that there should be a progressive decrease in the rate of growth from the lowest to the highest levels of any given marsh. This is not wholly true because at the lowest levels where there are bare or only partially seaweed- or plant-covered mud banks, the tide and waves are just as likely to wash away material as to deposit it. It is at the next stage, where there is a close cover of plants covered by all or by most high tides that upward growth is quickest. At higher levels the number of tidal inundations falls off, and so too does the rate of upward growth. These generalisations are well supported by measurements made in Wales, East Anglia and in Denmark. In all cases, a layer of some distinctive sand was put down in patches, about a metre square, at a series of stations along lines across the marshes. After the first covering high water, the sand was washed off the vegetation, and could be easily spread on the marsh surface, just as butter is spread on bread. If the stations were marked in some way, they could be inspected again after a period of years, and by carefully cutting through the newly accreted mud, the sand layer could be found and the amount of sediment accumulated on it measured. On the Norfolk marshes the rate was, on middle high marshes, of the order of a centimetre or less a year. In other places, such as on either side of the artificially controlled river mouths running into the Wash, it is much higher.

The upward growth of marshes is accompanied by other phenomena. It was stated above that at first the tidal waters cover the original sandflats with a sheet of water; as time goes on small mud banks and patches appear and the surface becomes more irregular. As the banks grow in area and in height, the tidal waters cease to ebb and flow as a sheet, but are broken up into channels, at first wide and ill-defined, but as the marsh continues to develop and vegetation spreads, the original surface is transformed into a green sward (in summer) cut up of numerous channels or creeks. The floor of the creeks is approximately the level of the original sand flats; the creek banks have been built up by accretion, sometimes (p. 54) much helped by wind-blown sand. The marsh surface may also be dotted with small shallow pools, called salt pans. If, as the marsh grows up, the vegetation spreads and thickens in such a way as to enclose a small area, the hollow or salt pan, which will be badly drained, will persist. If a small trench is made so that the water can run in and out of such a pan, it is only a matter of a season or two before it is covered with vegetation.

There are extensive salt marshes along the eastern sea-

board of the United States. D. W. Johnson (1925) described
these in rather more than general terms, and although much
more detailed work has been done on some of them since, we
cannot do better than to recall his main points. He distinguished three types. Type I, the New England type, occurs mainly
north of Boston. The outer zone of mud banks is colonised by
*Zostera*, the next and somewhat steeper zone is of soft mud
with a good deal of *Spartina glabra*, and the third and widest
zone, nearly horizontal, is a meadow in which *Spartina patens*
predominates. The top zone is only reached by high springs
and carries such plants as *Juncus* spp., *Scirpus americanus*,
and *Eleocharis rostellata*. These marshes are usually found at
the heads of bays and other sheltered areas. Type II he called
the Fundy type, after the bay of that name. They often consist
of bare reddish mud, locally carrying *Spartina glabra* and
*Statice*, spp. If they are enclosed by dykes or walls, they soon
develop into luxuriant salt meadows. Type III are the Coastal
Plain marshes. They are made of a blue mud 3–6 m thick. They
are grass-covered, mainly by *Spartina*, spp. They extend as far
as Florida, where they gradually give way to mangroves. The
American marshes are in many ways, perhaps superficial, unlike our own. The grasses grow much higher on some of them,
and the flowering plants which give such beauty to our own
marshes, especially in East Anglia, are far less conspicuous or
even absent.

The marshes on the continental coasts of the southern North
Sea in general resemble our own, and are well developed within
the Frisian Islands (the Wadden See), north-eastern Germany,
and western Denmark. The flats are usually much wider than
in this country; the tidal range is usually moderate, and in
many areas there has been extensive sedimentation. The plant
successions are to all intents and purposes like those in Great
Britain. In many parts the marshes are more sandy, and perhaps in general more like those of our western coasts. Zenkovich remarks that in the U.S.S.R. marshes are confined to the
northerly and north-easterly regions where climatic conditions
are harsh. They have not yet attracted much attention. In the
Gulf of Mezen' in the White Sea, it is interesting to note that

*Plantago maritima, Triglochin maritimum, Salicornia herbacea,* and *Aster tripolium* all occur.

The thickness of marsh deposits will naturally vary from place to place. If a piece of marshland coast is stable, the vertical thickness apart from that over any depressions in the floor on which it formed cannot exceed the extreme tidal range, and will probably be less, unless the marshes are very old. On a subsiding coast the thickness can, in theory, be considerable. But much will depend on the rate of subsidence relative to the supply of deposit. If the downward movement relative to sea-level is very slow, as it is on the Norfolk coast, the condition is to all intents and purposes similar to that on a stable coast; if it is rapid the marsh will be submerged. It is also important to know, or to estimate, the time during which marshes have been forming. Under certain circumstances they may form quickly and, at a guess – it is nothing more at this stage – all the north Norfolk marshes have probably been formed within the last 700 years, although some of them are known to have formed in the last 50–100 years. If in general this is true and (see pp. 82–100) if the downward movement relative to sea-level is very slow, it may follow that the marshes can thicken considerably. But at the same time the barrier beaches and spits behind which they have grown are, as a result of wave action, gradually encroaching upon them, so that it is possible to envisage the complete destruction of the marshes before they attain any great thickness. If, on the other hand, a marsh is forming on a slowly rising coast, it may extend seawards, but is not likely at any one place to attain appreciable thickness. Moreover, a barrier beach could under certain circumstances be built in front of it, and might have the effect of preserving what has already formed, or perhaps of cutting off any new supply, and so leading to its destruction. These are theoretical and tentative suggestions, but they may perhaps be worth while if they provoke thought or discussion about the age and stage of development of marshes.

The tropical equivalent of the salt marsh is the mangrove swamp. Along the mouths of many tropical rivers, and also along many alluvial coasts mangroves make thick forests. The trees may grow to a height of 40 ft or more, and the aerial roots form a dense and impenetrable layer at and a little above ground-level. Silt-laden waters penetrating the roots lead to some deposition, and the decay of the trees themselves presumably adds its quota. It is, however, wrong to assume that the mangroves 'make their own mud'. They spread out over a surface which may well be one of mud brought down by rivers. On the Queensland coast they may grow directly on the surface of reefs within the steamer channel. There is, I think, no doubt that once they have colonised a surface, especially one formed of mud or loose material, they stabilise it. In many parts of the north Queensland coasts they 'hold' ridges of coral shingle. Perhaps the most important species of mangrove along a coast is *Rhizophora mucronata*. It spreads by its long, bean-like seeds which float vertically in the water and sooner or later anchor themselves in some favourable spot. A small tree begins to grow and after a few years sends out its spread of aerial roots. Countless others are acting in a similar way and so the forest expands and renews itself. A mangrove swamp is usually penetrated by long channels, and there may also be large open spaces in it. Tidal currents in these channels may well be intensified but wave action is absent.

The other types of mangrove in or at the back of the swamps are *Avicennia* and *Bruguiera*. It is interesting to note that on the reefs in the steamer channel off Queensland, *Avicennia* is frequently found on the outside (seaward side) of the *Rhizophora*, and not landward of it as in a tropical river. The reason is the same in both cases; the outer parts of the reefs are somewhat higher than that on which the *Rhizophora* grows, and in a tropical estuary it is to be expected that the banks, where the *Avicennia* thrives, rise somewhat from river level.

# 4. Cliffs

Most of the more spectacular scenery of coasts is associated with cliffs. Yet a cliff is by no means easy to define. The best kind of definition is one like that used in the *Shorter Oxford English Dictionary* – a steep slope. If the slope faces the sea and if its foot is washed by the waves, it is all too often assumed that the one is the cause of the other. This, indeed, is often so, but we shall see later that several modifications of this simple view are necessary if we are to explain all cliffs.

If the sea comes to rest against a land mass – we are not here concerned with the way in which this occurs – the waves begin to work on the land, and if the original slopes do not plunge steeply down into deep water, erosion will begin and a notch will be cut in the land. This is the embryo cliff. A notch implies

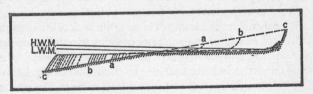

Fig. 12. *Embryo cliff.*

also a bench or platform (Fig. 12) in front of it. As time goes on this widens, and, assuming the land continues to slope upwards, the cliff will increase in height. It will be apparent that this evolution is likely to be much quicker in less resistant rocks; it may take a long time for even a small cliff to form in hard rocks.

The form that the cliff takes will vary according to local

factors. If the land is flat or rises but gently, the cliff may be fairly regular in height; if the land rises steeply then, clearly, the cliff form will accommodate itself to the nature of the slope. But the rocks forming the cliffs, whether resistant or otherwise, have structures of their own. If the beds are more or less horizontal, a well-jointed and well-bedded sedimentary rock will form a fairly vertical cliff. The joints are likely to be hollowed out, and as erosion proceeds, gullies will be cut, and stacks produced. If the bedding slopes seawards, the steepness of the cliff will depend largely on the angle of dip and the nature of the rocks, and this is also true if they dip *landwards*; in this case the cliff face is often stepped.

If, however, the bedding of the cliff is irregular, folded, or contorted, then the cliff form varies much in detail. Small-scale folding gives interesting local details; folding on a more general scale may give alternating vertical and sloping or horizontal beds. Since the beds themselves vary in their resistance to the waves, the harder ones stand out as buttresses or reefs, the softer form re-entrants, coves, and niches. If the sea has cut a marked bench in front of the cliffs, the corresponding features are seen in plan.

The general appearance of the cliffs, as already suggested, must depend a great deal on the nature of the land mass. Cliffs often have a fairly level top. This probably implies that the top surface, if within a few hundred feet of sea-level, was a former sea floor which has been uplifted. The noticeably flat top of the Carboniferous Limestone cliffs west of Tenby and of those in the Gower peninsula are examples. There are similar cliffs in Cornwall; the flat interior of the Lizard peninsula is a magnificent example of a raised sea floor. If, however, the coast is mountainous, then the cliffs may vary much in height and form. But here another points needs consideration. In mountain areas, and in others which are hilly, it does not follow that the whole cliff slope is of marine origin. Compare the cliffs of Exmoor with those of Pembrokeshire. In Exmoor there are long seaward slopes, only the lower part of which is steepened by the sea; in Pembrokeshire all the cliff appears to be sea-formed. Cliffs of the Exmoor type are often called

*Exmoor*

hog's-back cliffs. In more truly mountainous areas nearly all seaward slopes are only slightly modified by the sea, but other agents, e.g. glaciers, may have played a far more important part in modifying the nature of the coastal profile. On the west coast of Scotland it is often hard to say where the marine cliffs give way to those formed in some other fashion. For example, parts of the west coast of Rhum and Skye show magnificent sea cliffs, but it is difficult to claim a wholly or even part marine origin for some of the cliffs between Skye and Raasay and for the steep slopes in the Sound of Sleat. But one cannot be dogmatic. In many sheltered waters on the west coast of Scotland (see p. 95) there is evidence of marine erosion, perhaps more in the past than today, in places where wave action is greatly restricted. Along the outer parts of the major fiord coasts of the world the relative importance of marine and glacial erosion is by no means easily appreciated.

There is also another point of great interest to the cliff-walker. How far are the cliffs the work of the present sea? If we walk along the Holderness coast of Yorkshire, along the coast of Norfolk and Suffolk, or perhaps along most of the chalk cliffs and others cut in Cretaceous and Jurassic rocks in the south of England, we may be fairly certain that their form is wholly produced under present conditions. But even so, it is better to be guarded on this point for a reason that will shortly become clear. Along a good deal of Cardigan Bay, especially south of Aberystwyth, observation shows that in many places the cliffs are covered with a plaster of boulder clay; in places the old cliff is just exposed. In other places the cliffs are entirely free of boulder clay, and if those which are wholly or partially covered are discounted then one could easily assume that the uncovered ones are wholly formed under present-day conditions. The rocks forming the solid cliffs are, in Cardigan Bay, resistant, and those that are swathed in boulder clay are obviously of considerable age, either pre- or inter-glacial. The same is true of the rock bench in front of them. It is for this reason that we must have in mind the possibility that other rock benches and cliffs, where there is no boulder clay, are possibly of greater age than appears at first sight. Is the wide chalk bench around much of Thanet wholly formed under present conditions? It may be, but it is difficult to prove. This point will be reconsidered in Chapter 5, but we may say with confidence, that, for example, the magnificent rock platform, and in consequence the cliffs behind it, along much of north Devon and north Cornwall is not wholly formed under present conditions.

If the land mass is much dissected by rivers and other forms of land erosion, the coastline will be irregular. Lines of cliff alternate with river mouths and other inlets, and depending on the structures in the rock, the coast may be crenulate and picturesque. This type of coast is well seen in Cornwall, and there is an interesting general contrast between the more exposed northern and far western coasts, and the more sheltered south coast. Compare such a coast with that of Suffolk. There the coast is cut by several picturesque valleys which have been drowned so that salt water runs far inland up the Orwell, Deben, Alde and Yare. There are also several minor valleys which are now completely blocked by beach. But despite this considerable degree of dissection the coast of Suffolk is totally different from that of Cornwall. In Suffolk the cliffs offer no resistance to the sea, and erosion is serious, and the country inland is usually flat and not at all high.

Cliffs may be found in any type of rock. It will be convenient to make a broad distinction between those cut in igneous rocks and those in sedimentaries. Since Great Britain and Ireland contain such a great variety of rocks, most of the examples will be taken from our own islands.

Igneous rocks occur extensively in the western islands of Scotland. The most widespread, from the purely coastal point of view, is basalt which was poured out as lava flows. It is often cut by numerous dykes and sills of, mainly, dolerite. The dykes vary in width from a foot or so to several yards, and, as can be seen from Fig. 13, are associated with certain centres. They extend over great distances and are usually more resistant than the rocks they penetrate, so that on the coast they often stand out as ridges, resembling groynes. The reverse may also be true; some well-jointed dykes weather more rapidly

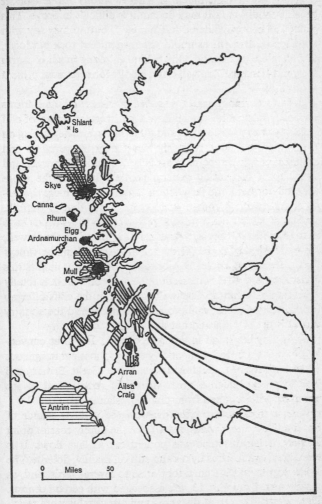

Fig. 13. *Tertiary igneous rocks in western Scotland. Horizontal shading = lavas; solid black = intrusive masses; lines = dykes; crosses = important sills. (From* The Evolution of Scotland's Scenery, *by J. B. Sissons. Oliver & Boyd, 1967.)*

than the country rock and form hollows or trenches. Dykes on
the foreshore are seen to perfection in the Ardnamurchan peninsula, the islands of Muck and Arran, and at the southern end
of the Kintyre peninsula. In the cliffs they often form buttresses,
and their effect will depend a good deal on the angle at which
they cut the cliffs. The great lava flows play a most important
role in the coastal scenery. In western Skye they build precipitous cliffs. The individual flows vary much in thickness; at
Talisker from 6 or 8 to 40 ft. In Dunvegan Head, about 1000 ft
high, there are 25 or more sheets. The coast between lochs
Bracadale and Brittle is wholly basaltic. The cliffs are high,
precipitous, and nearly vertical. Since they are formed of
separate flows they resemble stratified rocks, and both lavas and
sills often show magnificent columnar structure. On the eastern
side of Skye the basalts are seen to rest on Jurassic rocks. If the
basalts are more or less horizontal they give flat-topped features
like MacLeod's Tables near Dunvegan. Steeply inclined sills
give a vertical component to the scenery, and such formations
may give rise to detached masses and pinnacles standing out
from the general line of cliffs. Probably the best-known
examples of basaltic coastal forms are Fingal's Cave on the
island of Staffa, and the Giant's Causeway in Antrim. In both
these places, and in many others, the columnar nature of the
basalt is most striking. In England, basaltic or doleritic rocks
are uncommon on the coast; both at Dunstanburgh and Bam-
burgh castles in Northumberland the Whin Sill outcrops on the
coast and also reappears a few miles farther seaward to form the
Farne Islands.

On the east coast of Scotland, especially on both sides of the
Firth of Forth, igneous rocks contribute largely to the details of
the shore. The rocks are mainly the remains of old volcanic
vents, and usually give rise to lumpy and irregular masses on
the shore platforms which consist of bedded works of Carboniferous age. Locally the igneous rocks make interesting features; the Rock (= Distaff) and Spindle near St Andrews is
well known, and the cliffs at Dunbar harbour and Tantallon
castle are carved in them. These and the basalts stand in
marked contrast to the granites of Aberdeenshire, Land's End,

and the Isles of Scilly. Granite varies much within itself, but it frequently breaks up first into great cuboidal masses, separated by vertical and horizontal joints, and finally may produce much coarse sand. Cliff forms will therefore depend much upon the nature and inclination of the joints and on other lines of weakness. Some granites form castellated masses as at Land's End and Penberth. The Isles of Scilly are all part of a former great mass of granite which, before it was eroded and submerged, must have resembled Bodmin Moor or the other granite masses of Cornwall and Devon. Weathering of the granite in the Scillies has locally produced features resembling great blocks piled roughly one upon another. Some are hollowed out; sometimes rather spiky forms have been produced. The Aberdeen granite reaches the coast around Peterhead and forms steep and picturesque cliffs. Joints and other lines of weakness are etched out by the waves, but castellated forms are not conspicuous. Quarrying has locally been extensive and so the cliffs are not always natural in form.

Cliffs cut in sedimentary rocks vary greatly according to the nature of the rocks and to the movements which have affected them. It is out of the question to comment on all varieties of cliffs in bedded rocks, but certain rocks in Britain afford outstanding coastal scenery.

Along much of the east coast of Scotland and in Orkney the Old Red Sandstone outcrops over considerable distances. It is not only well developed but also easily inspected in Caithness. Inland Caithness is a rolling plateau and falls to sea-level in Sinclair's and Dunnett bays. Elsewhere it reaches the coast to form high and often vertical cliffs. The rock itself varies in composition; it may be conglomeratic and thickly bedded as between Ulbster and Sarclet, or it may occur in the form of flagstones as at Duncansby Head and Dunnett Head. For the most part the beds are nearly horizontal, and there is marked joining at right angles to the bedding. The sea erodes along these lines of weakness, but the rock is so resistant that the wearing away of the parts between the lines of weakness is extremely slow. Nevertheless, stacks and arches and also long narrow inlets, called geos, are cut along major joints or small

faults. Geos* have steep, parallel, and almost vertical walls, and
extend far into the cliffs which are often bordered by fine
stacks. The stacks near Duncansby Head are *c*. 200 ft high, and
form great pinnacles. They are cut in hard and tough flagstones, and rise from a narrow bench of marine erosion. Big
stacks, called cletts, may be 30 or more yards wide; a particularly fine example occurs at Holborn Head. Many stacks
still retain a covering of boulder clay or even peat; some are
cut through by caves, and look like heavy tables standing on
squat legs. It is worth noting that these stacks are all within
about 100 yards of the cliffs. There is another fine line of Old
Red cliffs north of Arbroath; they are perhaps less imposing
than those in Caithness, but are carved by the sea into a great
variety of forms – stacks, caves, geos, blow-holes. But here, as
elsewhere, the forms are not wholly produced under present
conditions; the Deil's Head, for example, must have been
formed when sea-level stood higher relative to the land. The
intricate nature of the cliffs is extremely well exemplified at
Dunnottar Castle.

Parts of the coast of New South Wales are fronted by magnificent cliffs cut in the Hawkesbury Sandstone. The coast
itself has had a complicated history in the sense that both
erosion and deposition during more than one relatively recent
change of sea-level have played an important part in its
present configuration. The beautiful inlet on which Sydney is
built is the finest, but only one of several similar features. Port
Jervis, about 100 miles south of Sydney, is enclosed between
two fine cliffed headlands which are former islands tied by
tombolos to the main coast. The cliffs on the northern headland are about 300 ft high, and vertical. Comparable cliffs,
varying in height and form with the structure of the rocks
extend over some distance, and are reminiscent of those in
eastern Caithness. But the great waves that break on parts of
the Australian coast have effects unknown in our islands. Bird

* Geos may well have a longer history than usually suggested. It is
not easy to see how the waves can make such clean-cut, narrow inlets
even along a fault or other line of weakness. It has been suggested by
Mr J. S. Smith of Aberdeen that the origin of geos may date back to a
period of climate different from that of the present.

remarks that near Port Campbell, in western Victoria, steep cliffs in Miocene rocks show platforms or ledges cut by waves *at the present sea-level* along bedding planes even 200 ft above high-water mark (*Coastal Landforms*, p. 48). In view of observations such as this, one cannot be too careful about making assumptions of changes of sea-level on the sole basis of platform height on exposed coasts.

Limestone affords distinctive inland scenery, and its appearance on the coast often reflects this since in many instances the intricate forms of caves and cliff sculpture are the result of the sea cutting into rocks formerly subjected to limestone weathering inland. This is, for example, true of some of the cliffs in the Tenby peninsula. In this and the Gower peninsula are perhaps the best examples of limestone cliffs in England. The cliffs are nearly vertical, the rock well bedded and jointed. Stacks, arches, caves and blow-holes are common, and the flat top (see p. 62) of the cliffs is a conspicuous feature. In the far north of Scotland there is a rather small but spectacular piece of limestone coast formed in rocks of Cambrian age; Smoo Cave forms a great gulley and is on a far larger scale than the Huntsman's Leap in the Tenby peninsula.

The coast of north-west county Clare from Black Head to Hag's Head, a distance of about 12 miles, is one of the most spectacular and interesting in Ireland (Fig. 14). It is particularly striking on account of the contrast between the bleached, terraced limestones of the Burren and the black, savage, perpendicular cliffs of Moher.

At Black Head, the north-west limit of the Burren Hills, the glacially scoured limestone scarp plunges steeply into the deep waters of Galway Bay. The scarp is broken in detail by bedding-plane steps, but slopes generally at 15°. This increases to 30° on the bold north face of Gleninagh Mountains and often to 90° at the very foot of the scarp where the present sea cliff is cut. From Black Head to Fisherstreet the modern cliff is seldom higher than 50 ft. It is usually formed in limestone, but is sometimes in indurated boulder clay. Corrosion by salt water has etched a foreshore of chaotic marine lapies* and has

* Limestone surfaces are often conspicuously furrowed and fretted as a result of the solvent action of acid waters.

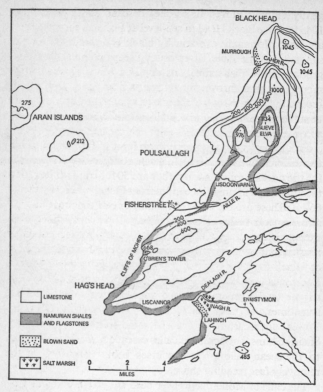

Fig. 14. *Part of the coast of western Eire near the Burren.*

so deeply penetrated joints that large, loosened, blocks of limestone are open to the attack of storm waves. The cliffs recede by natural quarrying of such blocks, and straight vertical sea walls result where dominant north–south joints run parallel to the shore. Cemented limestone till, almost as resistant as bedrock, forms a sub-vertical cliff on a limestone platform at Murrough, and marine stripping of drift at Poulsallagh has exposed striations on the underlying limestone. Since glacial striae seldom last long on limestone, their occurrence implies rapid marine erosion of the boulder clay. The gently dipping Burren limestones descend southwards from 1045 ft above Black Head to sea-level at Fisherstreet where they are uncomfortably overlain by black Namurian shales and sandstones. The Aille River usually seeps completely underground above Fisherstreet, its dry bed being blocked at its mouth by sand thrown up by waves and wind. But floods breach this barrier several times a year, and the surface stream then reaches the shore where it mingles with subterranean water ascending through sand and joints below high-water mark.

Fisherstreet strand is the southern limit of the Burren coast; thereafter black, menacing cliffs rise abruptly from the ocean for the next six miles. At first they are 50 ft high, but they soon reach 200 ft, and only three miles from Fisherstreet they rise to 668 ft. These are the cliffs of Moher, one of the most impressive elements in Irish coastal scenery. The cliffs, though extremely steep, are seldom perpendicular, because unequal resistance to erosion of the various shale and sandstone beds of which they are formed creates a slightly stepped profile. Enormous landslips and towering offshore stacks also contribute to the generally jagged appearance of the cliffs. But sometimes, as near the tourists' viewpoint at O'Brien's Tower, undercutting has caused some sections to overhang. Small streams that drain the shales cascade several hundred feet to the ocean below, their courses being truncated by the relatively fast receding shore.

The cliffs of Moher have never been studied in detail and no obvious evidence exists to indicate their age. Although their imposing bulk apparently presents a resistant barrier to the sea, the cliffs are fresh and subject to active erosion; their steepness being maintained by undermining. Such vigorous activity soon eradicates any morphological or depositional clues to the antiquity of the cliff line, and even the '25 ft' interglacial raised beach present to the north in Connemara and to the south in Kerry is not clearly distinguishable in this region.*

Chalk is a particular form of limestone, less resistant to

---

* This section on the cliffs of Moher has been contributed by Dr Paul W. Williams, who knows the district well. I am most grateful to him for allowing me to incorporate it in this book.

erosion than most other limestones such as the Carboniferous
Limestone. It is perhaps the most characteristic of our coastal
formations. Chalk is nearly always well bedded and well
jointed. The differences between the Upper, Middle and Lower
Chalk do not concern us, except to note that flints are absent
in the Lower Chalk. Along much of the Kent and Sussex coast
the chalk is nearly horizontal; it is steeply folded in the Isle of
Wight and in Purbeck. The Needles owe their resistance to
close folding of the chalk. Along much of the Dorset coast the
chalk dips steeply and is often crushed. Perhaps the finest chalk
cliffs in this country are those north of Flamborough Head in
Yorkshire. Flamborough Head itself at first sight looks very
unlike a typical chalk cliff, merely because it is thickly covered
with boulder clay which slopes at a much smaller angle, and is
also quite distinct in colour, from the chalk cliffs cut into
stacks, buttresses and small caves below. In some places chalk
cliffs are fronted by a wide platform; this is noticeably so in
east Kent and also off the Norfolk coast where the chalk under-
lies the glacial cliffs near the Runtons. Chalk cliffs fronted by a
fine platform are magnificently developed on the coast of
Picardy. In many places, especially in Kent, Sussex, the Isle of
Wight, and Dorset, the natural grassland on the summits of
the cliffs give particular character to the landscape. It is sometimes thought that the near verticality of chalk cliffs represent
a nice balance between sub-aerial and marine agents of erosion.
On the south coast, valleys cut in the chalk, and running in a
seaward direction, are now truncated by marine erosion so that
they hang above the beach. The valleys separating the Seven
Sisters cliffs just west of Beachy Head are perhaps the best-
known examples. It is necessary to add, however, that these
and similar valleys are now dry, and that they were probably
formed under climatic conditons different from those at present
prevailing.

In parts of north-western Scotland some of the most ancient
rocks in these islands reach the coast. The Lewisian gneiss is
perhaps best seen as a cliff form in the Outer Hebrides, but it
is only locally that it stands up as steep cliffs, e.g. between Gal-
lan Head and Aird Brevis on western Lewis. But in many

places the rock makes low and hummocky ground of a whitish-grey colour, without trees and showing abundant signs of severe glaciation. However, it also produces, as a result of submergence, a most irregular coastline, with many small islands and rocks. It is seen, in this respect, to perfection in Badcall Bay and between Kinlochbervie and Clashnessie. It is nearly always closely associated with the Torridon Sandstone, another pre-Cambrian rock which overlies the gneiss unconformably. As a rule the sandstone gives a softer landscape, and where the dip is seawards the cliffs are low, even insignificant. But occasionally it forms, like the Old Red Sandstone, fine cliffs, stacks, and headlands, as at the south end of Sandwood loch in western Sutherland. The great contrast between the steep and precipitous western sides and the low sloping eastern sides of Handa Island, Rhu Stoer, and Rhu More is explained by the dip of the rocks.

If the rocks forming the cliffs are strongly folded there is likely to be an infinity of detail in the cliff face. On some stretches of coast this can often only be properly appreciated from a boat, except in the few places where it is possible to get down to the beach. The coast between Hartland Point and Boscastle in north Devon and Cornwall is perhaps the most magnificent in Britain. It is for the most part formed of the Culm measures, which consist of alternating beds of shales and sandstones of Carboniferous age. There are numerous sharp anticlines and synclines, small faults, and many other phenomena displayed. The cliffs are fronted by a bench cut in the rocks so that although it may be difficult to see the cliff section, it is often easy to look down on this platform which gives in plan the sequence of rocks that the cliffs show in section. Usually the harder sandstones form reefs on the bench or buttresses in the cliffs, but this is not always the case. In places, as between Welcombe and Speke's Mill mouth, thick shale beds form prominent buttress reefs; this may perhaps be explained by the absence of joints, but the precise reason is uncertain. In some of the sharp anticlines the sea has cut small caves. This coast (see p. 74) is also characterised by numerous waterfalls. Another stretch of highly folded and contorted cliffs occurs on the coast of Berwickshire between Burnmouth and Cockburnspath. The Silurian rocks are intensely folded, and there is a great number of islands and skerries, caves, reefs, and stacks. St Abb's Head itself is a great mass of igneous rock (felstone). Once again, the details are best appreciated from a boat.

It would be easy to multiply these examples of cliff form from the many other exposures on our coast, but space will only allow reference to Pembrokeshire and part of Cardiganshire. The north coast of Pembrokeshire is very diversified, the cliffs are often spectacular, and there is an intricate dovetailing of igneous and sedimentary rocks. From Strumble Head to St David's all the headlands are igneous, and the inlets between are often cut in shales. But the igneous rocks vary considerably. In few other such short distances are variations in rock resistance to erosion so well shown – and this applies as much to macro- as to micro-structures. The south coast of the St David's peninsula of Pembrokeshire is one of the most beautiful in Britain. The rocks are mainly of Cambrian age, and the cliffs are often plant- or lichen-covered. The cliffs are steep, and the rock colours vary from purples to yellows and greys. Stacks and islets, caves and minor indentations abound, and Solva Harbour and Porth Clais are good examples of drowned valleys. In St Bride's Bay the cliffs are formed of newer rocks, Carboniferous and Old Red Sandstone. The variation in form and colour of the cliffs on the south side of the bay, and the westward continuation of the peninsula, known as the Deer Park, into the volcanic islets of Skomer, Midland and, farther south, the island Grassholm and the cliffs in Marloes Bay make an unforgettable scene. The Tenby peninsula is referred to on page 62.

COASTAL WATERFALLS

Water, in the form of small streams falling over a cliff, is a common phenomenon, and in many cases does not call for any special comment. Often it means that the sea has cut back the cliffs more than the stream has cut down its bed. The small stream in Fairlight Glen, near Hastings, is an instance. In Skye there are some fine coastal waterfalls which drain from lochs and plunge vertically over cliffs formed in basalt flows, which, on the eastern side of the island, rest on Jurassic beds. The stream flowing from Loch Mealt is well known, but there are also many others in Bearreraig, and in Loch Bracadale, and at Talisker, on the other side of the island. But in Britain the most interesting waterfalls are between Westward Ho! and Boscastle. The watershed runs close to and nearly parallel with the coast. The falls vary a good deal in nature, and depend much upon whether the stream drains a flat topped or a sloping cliff—i.e. a hog's-back cliff. In general, the former are far more spectacular than the latter. Litter Water has a vertical fall of 75 ft; Milford Water consists of five individual falls: the uppermost is a dip fall which at its foot turns at a right angle to follow a gutter, then another turn leads to a steep fall running contrary to the dip, and below are two smaller falls. Some of the falls – there are more than 30 – have been altered or even obliterated by landslips; others flow down steeply inclined slopes, and some streams, e.g. Wargery Water, used to flow for a short way parallel with the cliff top before they fell over as a fall. Marine erosion, however, has cut into their courses, sometimes more than once, so that now they plunge over the cliff some distance upstream from the original fall. One of these former courses, without, however, any stream at the present time, is the well-known Valley of the Rocks near Lynton.

## LANDSLIPS

Among the phenomena that locally give character to cliffed coasts is the landslip. Slips can occur in very different types of rock. In this section we shall be concerned with those of some size and not with cliff falls or slips of a minor nature. There are several good examples in Britain; the best known, Dowlands, is on the Devon and Dorset boundary. The great chasm was formed in 1839. The 18 months previous to the slip had been wet, and the major slip occurred on Christmas night. 'During December 26th, the land that had been cut off by the fissures in the cliff top gradually subsided seawards, and by the evening had reached a position of equilibrium in the undercliff. A new inland cliff, 210 feet high in its central position and sinking to east and west, had then been exposed, backing a chasm into which some twenty acres of land had subsided. The length of the chasm was about half a mile, while its breadth increased from 200 feet on the west to 400 feet on the east.' (Arber, *Proc. Geol. Ass.*, **51**, 1940, 257.) Many other slips had doubtless preceded this one, and minor ones have taken place at other localities in the area. The cause of the slip depends on the seaward dip of the beds. Where the junction of the Upper Greensand (mainly sand and sandstones) and the underlying Gault clay slope seawards, the erosion caused by the waves cutting into the face of the cliff removes their outward support so that the upper beds slide over the lower.

The Isle of Wight also affords some good examples. In the Solent coast the Hamstead beds are locally in a constant state of flow. Near St Catherine's Point, in the south of the island, the inner and high vertical cliff is found in the Upper Greensand rocks, but much has slipped forward on the underlying Gault clay to form tumbled ground and the present cliffs. Some of those slips are very old, others quite recent. Farther east, between Folkestone and Dover, is another area of major slips which form Folkestone Warren. They have been investigated by W. H. Ward (*Geogrl J.*, **105**, 1945, 170) whose sections show that the slips owe their origin to the erosion by the sea of the Gault. Moreover, the slips are rotational, in the sense that they turn about a horizontal axis. It seems that the plane on which the slipping takes place passes through the whole thickness of the Gault, and it is not thought that the Chalk is merely slipping over the Gault. Ward also suggests that the Dowlands slip was also rotational. Folkestone Warren forms a distinct undercliff between Folkestone and Dover, and presents serious problems to British Railways, whose main line follows the strike of the slip.

Zenkovich discusses some interesting examples which have been investigated in the Black Sea. Two types are distinguished (see Fig. 15). The major ones occur when the slip plane originates in clays of Miocene age, the top of which is slightly above sea-level. Slides of this type involve the whole of the superjacent rocks, parts of which may break up into large

Plate I. *Scolt Head Island, 1964. (Ministry of Defence Air Force Department photograph: Crown copyright reserved.)*

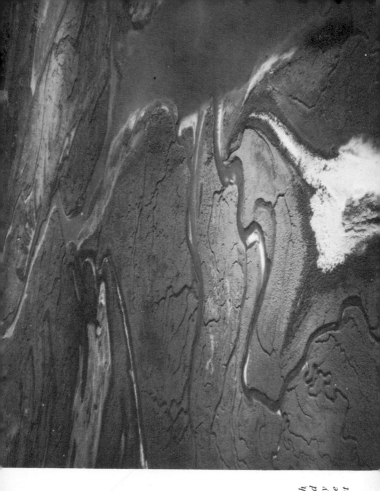

Plate II. *Details of salt marsh topography, Scolt Head Island (Lower Hut Marsh). (Photo by J. K. St Joseph, Cambridge University Collection: copyright reserved.)*

Plate III. *Drumlins in Clew Bay, Ireland. Drowned features of glacial deposition. (Photo by J. K. St Joseph, Cambridge University Collection: copyright reserved.)*

Plate IV. Above: *Ro Wen: the spit at the mouth of the Mawddach Estuary, Wales.* Below: *The Bar, near Nairn. (Photos by J. K. St Joseph, Cambridge University Collection: copyright reserved.)*

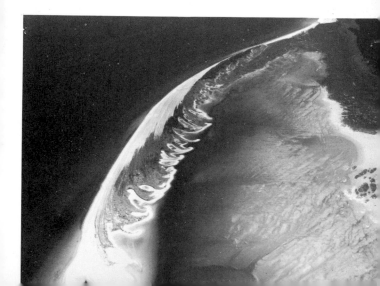

Plate V. Above: *Fowey, Cornwall: a drowned river mouth.* Below: *Coastal landslip and undercliff, Rocken End, Isle of Wight.* *(Photos by J. K. St Joseph, Cambridge University Collection: copyright reserved.)*

Plate VI. *Coastal landslip, near Culverhole Point, Devon. (Photo by J. K. St Joseph, Cambridge University Collection)*

Plate VII. *The Cliffs of Moher, Ireland. (Photo by J. K. St Joseph, Cambridge University Collection: copyright reserved.)*

Plate VIII. Above: *The Carboniferous Limestone cliffs near Lydstep, and Caldy Island in the background (South Wales).* Below: *Cliffs of Old Red Sandstone, Kincardineshire, Scotland. (Photos by J. A. Steers.)*

Plate IX. Above: *The Bow Fiddle Arch cut in thick-bedded quartzite and thin mica-schist, Scar Nose, Portknockie. (Photo by J. A. Steers.)* Below: *The Rock and Spindle, a volcanic formation near St Andrews. (Crown copyright Geological Survey photograph. Reproduced by permission of the Controller H.M. Stationery Office.)*

Plate X. Erosion and depletion of beach on the Lincolnshire coast in the storm surge of 1953. (Photo by J. A. Steers.)

Plate XI. The (Patella) raised beach platform, near Lannacombe, Devon. (Photo by J. A. Steers.)

Plate XII. Above: *Stephen's Island, Queensland: bench on lee side very near high-water mark.* Below: *Hope Islands, Queensland: young mangroves colonising reef flat. (Photo by M. A. Spender.)*

blocks. This process may cause ridges to bulge up in the sea
bed. The other type of slide affects only the loess and Quaternary clays, and these may not even reach the sea. As a result of
these various slides the whole coastal slope, about 300 metres
wide and backed by a cliff about 40 metres high, forms a
rough and tumbled surface. There are also excellent examples

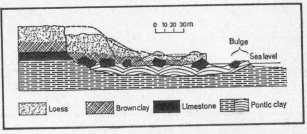

Fig. 15. *Diagrammatic profile of a landslip near Odessa.
(From A. M. Drannikov in Zenkovich, op. cit.)*

of flowing landslides in the Crimea. Along parts of the coast,
water from limestone areas is discharged in channels at the
foot of the limestone plateau, and percolates into clay-shales
below. These shales, when saturated, become capable of flow,
and over long periods of time individual flows erode their
beds and carry seawards all the material which has gathered
in them. But the upper layer of the landslip area, where it is
protected by limestone fragments, may be so slightly affected
by erosion of surface water, that a kind of inverted relief is
formed – permanent streams cut deep valleys and the land-
slipped material may form watersheds between the streams.

There is every gradation between major landslides and the
more or less constant loss along certain cliffs caused primarily
by land water draining out of them. This is particularly well
illustrated in most boulder clay cliffs. Those between Weybourne and Happisburgh on the Norfolk coast illustrate the
process very well, especially in the Cromer–Sheringham area.
Here the glacial deposits are of more than one age, and the
second ice advance caused a good deal of disturbance and

minor folding and contortions in the older. Moreover, the deposits vary greatly. Some parts of the cliffs may consist of stiff boulder clay; elsewhere the proportion of sand and gravel is high and clay may be almost absent. The water draining out from the land above gives rise to small slips, and the top edge of the cliffs is characteristically scalloped. Slips can locally take place more easily down the seaward-facing limb of a small fold or contortion. The fallen material gathers at the cliff foot, and until it is removed by the sea, forms a temporary protection to the cliff.* The same kind of process occurs on the long line of boulder clay cliffs south of Flamborough Head and elsewhere. Even in fine summer weather there is a constant, if small, loss on cliffs of this sort. Sand and fine stones are continually falling down. In the aggregate the amount of material produced in this way is far from negligible, although it becomes lost in the bigger falls.

Masses of cliff are likely to break away from time to time in almost any rock but the changes produced in this way are not great, although a particular fall may appear spectacular. In relatively resistant rocks these falls are probably mainly caused by the undercutting of the sea, and have occurred, for example, in Beachy Head. In the more resistant rocks of Devon and Cornwall, and around much of the coasts of Scotland, slips are comparatively rare.

There is another type of cliff that needs to be mentioned – the so-called plunging cliffs. In some places the land drops steeply down into deep water and there is no, or very little, evidence of a bench cut in them at or just below sea-level. The great cliffs of western Hoy (Orkney) and some of those in western Ireland are probably of this type. Wave action may be very vigorous, but the waves may be reflected from the cliffs and fail to cut a bench or platform. Are the cliffs of marine or some other origin? It is difficult to envisage a simple origin as a result of wave erosion, and one is tempted to think that in

---

* The visitor to these cliffs must not expect always to see all the phenomena described. Erosion is severe and the cliffs vary so rapidly that the cliff face today may be very unlike that six months ago or six months ahead.

some cases at least the land and sea have been brought together along some great structural line, a major fault perhaps. Post-glacial rise of sea-level is also an important factor, perhaps the most important, in the production of plunging cliffs.

Some lines of cliffs given the impression of having been formed by faulting. It is, however, difficult to prove this. Certain coastlines have, in the past, been outlined by movements of this type, but since the faulting occurred not only have many other tectonic movements taken place, but also shifts of sea-level in glacial and possibly earlier, times and there has also been a considerable amount of sub-aerial denudation. Other more complicated histories may have taken place, such as the covering by sediment of an old faulted area by deposition under an ancient sea followed by a new uplift, and a re-exposure of the faults as a result of later sub-aerial erosion. There is no need to elaborate this theme; all that needs to be emphasised is that in almost all cases what appears to be a fault coast has had a long history, and at best the cliffs of such a coast represent the work of marine and terrestrial denudation over a long period of time, so that the evidence, if any, of the faulting is indirect and often obscure.

Cotton, who has described and explained many features of the coasts of New Zealand, draws particular attention to the scarp of the Wellington fault in Port Nicholson. The north-western part of that inlet is bordered by a remarkably straight and uniform cliff, dissected by some transverse valleys (cf. p. 72). Wave action is limited. In 1912 Cotton argued in favour of the youth, the newness, of this scarp, but subsequent work has made it clear that its evolution has been far more complicated (*Trans. R. Soc. N.Z.*, **84**, 1957, 761). Earthquakes (p. 83) may produce small fault scarps on a coast, and if in resistant rocks they may persist. But Cotton very properly points out: 'Some young fault scarps [may] form true lines of cliff facing the ocean, but few statements that these exist have been substantiated by critical discussion of examples. ... On the island of Alinnia, in the mobile Dodecanese region, Migliorini has, however, found young rectilinear fault scarps facing the sea as cliffs. These now "plunge" as a result of drowning ascribed to local subsidence of the island, though alternatively the drowning may be eustatic. . . . Plunging cliffs apparently of similar origin form the straight west sides of the islands of Santa Cruz and Angel de la Guarda and the east side of Ceralto Island, in the Gulf of California. . . .' (Cotton, *N.Z. Geogr.*, **8**, 1952, 49.)

Before closing this chapter it will be convenient to say something of the rate of erosion in various parts of the coast. In resistant rocks change takes place very slowly; every now and again large blocks may be dislodged, a slip may occur, but measurable change is rare. This in itself causes one to think about the origin of such cliffs. Just how did Devon and Cornwall attain this present form? How long have these cliffs been in process of formation? Have the cliffs been cut back – both the present and the older cliffs associated with the raised platforms – from a once sloping surface, or did the area come into being as a great horst? Do the platforms along the Hartland area only imply a retreat of the cliffs from the outer edge of the platforms? So many questions of the sort are easy to pose, but almost impossible to answer.

Chalk cliffs, often vertical possibly because of a nice balance between marine and sub-aerial erosion, may show perceptible retreat in a matter of decades or even more quickly in some places. The same is true of cliffs or relatively non-resistant limestones and sandstones such as occur in north Yorkshire or in Dorset. Much may depend upon the dip of the beds, and a great deal on the sequence of beds. The great landslips of Axmouth and Folkestone are closely associated with clay beds beneath sandstones and chalk. But erosion on a spectacular scale is usually limited to incoherent sands and gravels and such deposits as boulder clay. The long line of boulder clay cliffs between Bridlington and Spurn Head have retreated more rapidly than any other in Britain. It is estimated on fairly reliable grounds that along this stretch of 34 miles about 83 square miles have disappeared since Roman times. On many parts of this stretch 5 to 6 ft are lost annually. The cliffs vary slightly in height: 30–40 ft is perhaps a fair average. The glacial cliffs near Sheringham and Cromer on the Norfolk coast show a similar retreat. Locally they are higher than those in Holderness, and do not stand so steeply. In cliffs of this sort, land water draining out through them may often play as important a role as the sea. The irregular structure and very mixed character of the cliffs often lead to slips and slumping from above, so that the top edge of the cliffs is scalloped. The fallen material collects on the beach and, whilst there, protects the cliffs from sea erosion until it is removed by the waves. It is often quite difficult to see a clean face over all these cliffs. In Suffolk, bedded sands and gravels form attractive but rapidly eroded cliffs. Throughout history Dunwich has suffered, and nothing remains of the mediaeval town. Houses built on the cliffs top in 1935 a little north of Southwold had to be pulled down in less than 30 years because the sea had removed a wide field in front of them. The cliffs hereabouts are 30–40 ft high. Farther north, near Covehithe, where the cliffs drop to 10–12 ft, 80 ft was removed in the great surge of 1953.

There is still a great deal of scope for anyone who is interested in the form and evolution of cliffs. In this chapter some of the more important features have been noted, but it cannot be emphasised too strongly that each and every line of cliff presents its own peculiar problems. Mention has been made of hog's-back cliffs; in Cardigan Bay a particular form called a bevel is found. Alan Wood (*Lpool and Manchr geol. J.*, **2**, 1959, 371) has shown that although in some ways it resembles the hog's-back form, its association with ledges or flats implies that there have been vertical movements, since two or even three terraces may be found. Careful observation elsewhere may easily lead to the discovery of phenomena which will throw more light on cliff development. Anyone, professional or amateur, will do well to ponder the nature and origin of the cliffs along the top of which he may be walking. Ordinary textbook explanations are for the most part quite inadequate.

# 5. Vertical Movements

Along almost any length of coast throughout the world one can find some trace or indication of vertical displacement having taken place, probably in recent geological times. The movements may have been produced by a change of sea-level, that is to say by an actual increase or decrease in the total volume of water in the oceans, or by movements of the land, or by a combination of both processes. The most likely cause of a volumetric fluctuation of the oceans is the oncoming of a glacial period, or the recovery from one. The growth of extensive ice caps implies that the moisture which gave birth to them came from the oceans. It is generally conceded that when the ice caps of the Quaternary were at their maximum the ocean level was lowered about 300 ft. Since the Quaternary glaciation was punctuated with inter-glacial periods, the ocean level must have fluctuated considerably. If only ocean level measurements of this sort, i.e. eustatic movements, were involved the problem would be relatively simple since it follows that if nothing else happened the changes of level would be the same at every part of the world facing open water.

Unfortunately, simple eustatic movements are nearly always accompanied by land movements. The formation of the great ice caps meant that the land area on which they rested was heavily weighted and depressed. There is no need to discuss the structure of the earth's interior, but it can be taken for granted that an area depressed by the weight of an ice cap would, to some extent, affect also the surrounding areas, because of the peripheral translocation of material that takes place in the sub-crystal layers. This, in its turn, implies that there may be some bulging, or upward movement, in the crust on the margin of an ice cap. When the ice melts, a reverse process will take place; the former sub-glacial area will rise and the peripheral parts will sink. These movements will all take place slowly, and their effects will continue to be felt long after the ice has disappeared. It follows from what has been said that in some parts of the globe both movements may be going on together. For example, we know that much of the Scandinavian peninsula is still rising, whereas south-east England and the southern parts of the North Sea are sinking. There are similar oscillations taking place in the north-eastern parts of North America. If, at any place, the rise of sea-level eustatically takes place at the same rate as the upward, isostatic, movement of the land, there will be no apparent change of level in the coast; on the other hand if upward isostatic movement exceeds the eustatic, there will clearly be an actual rise of land relative to the sea, and vice versa if the downward movements brought about isostatically cause a submergence of the land.

Apart, however, from movements of sea-level directly connected with the ice, there are others. There may be in the course of ages marked alterations in the form of the ocean basins which will be reflected in coastal changes. On a smaller scale earthquakes and vulcanicity often produce significant effects on the coast. The earthquake in Yakutat Bay, Alaska, 1899, led to changes of level on the coast of as much as 140 feet. The disastrous Japanese earthquake of 1923 produced profound changes in the submarine topography of Sagami Bay. The great eruption of Krakatoa in 1883 blew away about half the island of Rakata, and built up neighbouring small islands and, by the deposition of solid matter ejected from the volcano, the sea floor for a considerable distance around the cone was built up. Renewed movements along lines of fault may occur. Since, however, they are usually accompanied by earthquakes or tremors they do not make a separate category.

Although there are other ways in which the volume of oceanic water may be affected, they are not of such a nature to affect our particular problem.

How, then, do these movements show themselves on a coast? In Chapter 2 it was shown how a beach is formed, and that it

rests on a bench cut by wave action. If therefore beaches or
wave-cut benches are found above present sea-level, they
clearly imply that some change of level has taken place. It is
not rare to find that two or more such features, forming a
staircase, may occur. It will be apparent that if this is so the
the highest is likely to be the oldest. But another point demands
consideration. If beaches are stepped, the implication is that
there was a time interval, probably of some considerable
length, separating any pair of beaches. But why should this be
so? Both eustatic and isostatic movements are presumably
continuous, so it is difficult to see why there should not be a
gradual grading of one beach into another. It should be noted
at this stage that the terms raised beach and wave-cut bench
are often used as if they were synonymous. Strictly, a raised
beach means that true beach deposits occur, but as they are
often associated with a bench the terms are generally used as if
they were interchangeable. It is nevertheless true, that a bench
takes far longer to form than does a beach deposit on its
surface.

At many localities the coast may take the form of a flat
plateau faced by cliffs. The surface of the plateau may well be a
former sea floor and its present position implies considerable
changes in the relative levels of land and sea. Reference to
pages 62 and 69 shows that such surfaces are particularly well
developed in parts of South Wales and in Cornwall. These
surfaces are older than the raised beaches, *sensu stricto*, and
are mainly of Tertiary age. They also must have taken much
longer to form than the narrower raised benches.

If the land has been partially drowned by change of sea-level
the features produced are also indicative of this change. On
many beaches of Great Britain and other countries expanses
of peat are often visible at low tides. Examination of those
deposits may reveal fallen trees or other traces of a dry land
flora. If these deposits are extensive there is little doubt that
they have been lowered relative to sea-level. Caution, however,
is necessary because erosion of the sea may lead to flooding of
a lowlying area, the death of the vegetation, and the production of what, at first sight, seems a typical submerged forest.

On the other hand, where excavations have been made for docks or other coastal works, it has frequently been observed that there are several peat beds at lower levels underlying the surface one. In such cases there is absolute proof of change of level.

The general appearance of a line of coast is often the clearest indication of a change of level. Strongly indented coasts in which the sea runs up creeks and inlets, giving a drowned appearance, take various forms such as the fiords of Norway, the sea lochs of Scotland, the rias of south-western Ireland, Pembrokeshire, and Brittany, and the not uncommon accompaniment of numerous off-shore islands, rocks, and skerries that have been formed by the sea submerging former valley systems, some of which may have been glaciated. The melting of the great ice sheets must naturally have given rise to submergence, and only those coasts along which the isostatic uplift of the land has been of major importance would show counterbalancing effects, although these would not necessarily eliminate the effects of submergence. This matter is also discussed in Chapter 6. In striking contrast to deeply indented and rocky coasts, are the flat alluvial coasts which are often fringed by barrier beaches (see pp. 32, 36) seen to perfection around the Gulf of Mexico and the eastern United States south of New Jersey. Much of the north Siberian coast also seems to be of this type. Coasts of this type are by no means necessarily raised sea floors. The history of the Atlantic seaboard of the U.S.A. is complicated, and clearly both elevation and depression relative to sea-level have taken place. The Fall Line is an old cliff, but inlets like those of the Chesapeake and Delaware, and many others point to a later submergence, but the full explanation is far more complicated. It is usually implied in textbooks that a raised sea floor will give a lowlying coast of simple outline. This is certainly not always the case. In those parts of the world where the continental platform is well developed, an emergence will probably give a flat coast. If we suppose that the North Sea floor were to be exposed we should indeed have a coast of this sort, but it would not be so if the sea floor between Scotland and the Outer Hebrides were laid bare. It may be argued that some smoothing could occur during the process, which is not likely to be a rapid one, but it is improbable that it would have marked effects in areas of resistant rocks.

Are there any stable areas on the coastlines of the world which allow us to regard them as standards to which movement may be referred? As long ago as 1911 General de Lamothe discussed the platforms on the coast of Algeria, and suggested that similar levels would be found in Provence. Depéret's investigations showed that there was some correlation, and further work in the Mediterranean and in western France followed. There is reason to think that some reasonable degree of correlation exists between these regions, and that this part of the globe may have been tolerably stable since Sicilian times. However, much of the Mediterranean has been affected by tectonic movements associated with earthquakes and volcanoes, so it is impossible to extend the assumed stable area with any confidence. The highest of the Mediterranean terraces, the Sicilian (*c.* 300 ft) is above any level that can reasonably be supposed for high sea-levels associated with the Ice Age. The lower ones, Milazzian, *c.* 200 ft, Tyrrhenian, *c.* 100 ft, and the Monastirian, *c.* 50 ft, could conceivably be explained in this way. However, the assumed stability of the Algerian and neighbouring coast is in some doubt, and many geomorphologists are reluctant to accept as Pleistocene sea-levels more than about 100 metres above the present sea.

It is difficult to base views on the assumed stability of any land area. E. C. Bird's reference to Australia is relevant: 'Australia is thought to have become a relatively stable continent when the late Tertiary movements came to an end, but tectonic deformation continued on parts of the coast into Pleistocene and even Recent times. On the south-east of South Australia the Mount Gambier region has risen, and the area round the mouth of the Murray has subsided. In Victoria, Port Phillip Bay occupies a tectonic depression, or sunk land, bordered on the eastern side by Selwyn's Fault, an active fault along which earthquakes still occur from time to time: the

Mornington earthquake of 1932 was traced to a displacement along this fault. Farther east the South Gippsland Highlands have been elevated while adjacent lowlands, such as the synclinal drained by the Latrobe River, have subsided. These movements may still be in progress. Compared with Victoria, the New South Wales and east Queensland coasts are thought to have been relatively stable since the uplift of the Eastern Highlands came to an end, but further investigation may well modify this supposition. Coasts bordering the shield area of Western Australia are also thought to have been stable through Quaternary times, but it is probable that tectonic deformation has continued in Recent times around Exmouth Gulf, in the far north-east. Little is known of the Quaternary stability of Australia's northern coasts.' This long quotation, from one who has studied Australian coasts, is important since it emphasises the difficulty, even the impossibility, of making any assumption of coastal stability. What is true of Australia is probably true of Africa and eastern South America. In short, we must be content with the detailed study of areas or small regions. Until far more has been done in this way, reliable correlations on a world scale are out of the question.

This does not, however, rule out the possibility that in the last six thousand years, since the oceans are assumed to have attained their present general level, there may have been small oscillations which have left evidences at accordant heights in many parts of the world. Fairbridge, off western Australia, finds evidence for stands at 10–12 ft, 5–6 ft, and 2–3 ft. My own observations on the Queensland coast, made in 1928 and 1936, and now requiring detailed checking, support this, although levels may be a little different from those elsewhere on account of differences in tidal range and other factors. But even if in the non-glaciated regions some general correlation of these recent changes is possible, there is as yet no convincing means of relating these to features in the glaciated areas.

So far what has been said implies the correlation of beaches mainly by height. There are other means, but they apply perhaps better to the older and well preserved beaches which contain fossil shells. To use this method with assurance implies that the fossils are well known and that comparisons of one locality with another can be made with confidence. Moreover, the nature of the fossils is also an indication of temperature conditions of the sea, and so they certainly give us useful information. The Arctic fauna associated with the so-called 100-ft beach of Scotland (p. 89) and the warmer fauna of the later and badly named 25-ft beach are instances. But in a vast continent relatively so little is known that it is easy to fall into serious errors. In recent years a new tool has been used – the dating of shells, wood, coral fragments, etc., by means of radio-carbon measurements. It is a good method in deposits of 30 000 years old or less, but it is essential to make sure that the object dated was incorporated in the beach where it was forming, and not at some later date. There is little doubt that in future this and other methods will allow a much closer correlation of beaches in different areas.

But what is meant by the height of raised beach or bench? It is only too easy to say that a certain feature is 100 ft above the present sea. Does 'present sea' mean high water, mean tide level, or low water? If so how was the assumed datum obtained? In a well-mapped country it is possible to refer a beach to Ordnance Datum or whatever fixed level may be used. But over vast areas of the globe this is impossible. Local mean, high, or low water level may be obtained approximately if the investigator has suitable equipment and is in a given locality for at least a lunar month. This, however, is often out of the question, and so reference must be made to some local datum. On the Queensland coast I found that the upper level of the rock oyster (*Ostrea mordax*) coincided closely with the upper level of neap tides. Other field workers have used similar evidence. But the necessity of a datum is only part of the problem. A marine bench has a slight seaward slope; a beach deposit may have been piled up by storm waves and so caused to represent an unusually high level. It may be apparently easy to see the general level of a bench, but at what part should its height be measured? In the past there have been far too many rough estimates, or heights measured in wrong places. For a wave-cut bench it is now generally agreed that the angle where bench and cliff meet is probably best, although talus and vegetation may often make it difficult to do this.

For a built terrace, a shingle foreland such as Dungeness, the top of the outer edge represents the height of effective wave action. It is far more difficult to measure the height of a barrier island formed of sand since wind action and vegetation may make any upper limit of wave action somewhat difficult to find. It is essential to have these practical points and difficulties in mind in addition to reading the extensive literature on the subject. There are so many statements of the nature that a bench 'varies in height from 50 to 70 ft' (or even a greater range); what does this mean? It may mean, as D. W. Johnson long ago pointed out, that the inner edge of the beach is 20 ft higher than the outer, or that the variations on its general surface are as much as 20 ft, or perhaps that when followed parallel to the coast it slopes downwards at 20 ft in a given distance. Whatever the difficulties faced by an investigator in the field, he should do all he can to make clear, without any shadow of doubt, precisely what his measurements signify. Allowance must also be made for tidal conditions. It is by no means certain at what level a bench is cut; to some extent it must depend on tidal range, so care must be taken in relating benches in places where the range is low or effectively nil, as in much of the Caribbean, to those where the range is considerable. Some allowances must also be made for the relative resistance or rocks of different types, and also for the arrangement of the rocks on the coast. Horizontally bedded rocks of medium resistance are likely to give well-developed benches; rocks dipping toward the sea, especially if somewhat resistant, are likely to give poor benches. The reader can easily picture other types for himself.

Since evidences of change of level are worldwide it will be convenient to examine only one or two particular places in order to illustrate the nature and complexity of the problem. Great Britain affords an admirable instance of this. For many years – and even today – we have spoken of the (1) pre-Glacial beach of the south of England, (2) the 100-ft beach of parts of the west and north-east of Scotland, (3) the so-called 50-ft beach of Scotland, and (4) the post-Glacial 25-ft beach. It was early recognised that these beaches are not always at 100, 50, or 25 ft above sea-level, yet the names persist. Nothing could be more misleading than to continue these names, but it is often extremely difficult to avoid referring to them, and thus keeping in mind the ideas of height that they suggest. It must also be remembered that a great deal of the pioneer work on raised beaches and associated phenomena originated in this country, and that field geologists of the Geological Survey, working in different places and seeing only limited extents of beach could not be expected to do more than record what they saw. Moreover at that time modern ideas on glacio-eustasy did not exist. It is, therefore, to the credit and far-sightedness of W. B. Wright, also of the Geological Survey, that he first began to see some overall pattern in our beaches. He, however, did not make detailed measurements of their height, but he did realise that a marked bench cut in resistant rocks may not be wholly of one age.

We have made clear that the problem of raised beaches and buried peat beds is one and the same. It was Godwin's magnificent work in the East Anglian fens that showed the prime importance of careful and detailed measurements. With the archaeologists, especially Grahame Clarke, he established the presence or Tardenoisian, Neolithic A, and Neolithic B occupation levels in the fens, the traces of which are now deeply buried. Hazzledine Warren on the Suffolk–Essex coast and A. G. Smith in the Humber fenlands have extended this work. We can now trace the history and development of many of these and similar areas by means of these researches. The problem of the raised beaches, however, remains unsolved in any comprehensive sense. Donner began to make some detailed measurements in western Scotland, but only at 30 sites. This number was quite insufficient to enable proper deductions to be made for Highland Scotland as a whole. It is to McCann and Sissons,* working in different parts of Scotland, that we must turn for a much fuller understanding. McCann was con-

---

* *Trans. Inst. Brit. Geogrs.* No. 39, 1966 (Special Numbers), and see p. 92.

cerned with the coast between Loch Broom and the Firth of Lorne, and made 191 height measurements. Sissons and his colleagues working in the Firth of Forth and neighbouring districts have made many hundreds of borings in the carse and related deposits, and have interpreted the later and post-Glacial history of the area in great detail. Work of this sort takes time and may be somewhat tedious, but it is essential if we are going to reach correct conclusions.

Let us now return to the main raised beaches of Britain. Along the south coast and around the Bristol Channel there are many traces of beaches and benches at about 10 ft above present high water mark. (Precise measurements of height have not been made.) It used to be called the pre-Glacial beach, but it is far better to forget this name and call it the *Patella* (limpet) beach, since this shell is commonly found in the deposits. '*Pre-*' Glacial must also disappear. It was fully discussed by Wright who pointed out that the beach or bench is frequently covered by head, a solifluction deposit sludging down from the high ground when southern Britain was experiencing a peri-glacial climate. There are some magnificent remains of bench and head near Prawle Point in south Devon. But a solifluction deposit on a bench does not necessarily imply a *pre*-glacial age for the bench; solifluction would have taken place in the inter-glacial periods, a point fully appreciated by Wright. This has now been proved by some detailed work by Arkell at Tre-betherick Point at the mouth of the river Camel. Here the beach is covered by various deposits, including head, but the important point to emphasise is the well-preserved nature of the beach, a point difficult to explain if it really of pre-glacial age. The dating of the oldest deposits on it make it seem more than probable that they belong to the Riss glaciation and therefore that the beach is of Mindel-Riss, i.e. second inter-glacial, age. The *Patella* beach also occurs in South Wales and has been investigated by George* in the Gower peninsula. There are also traces of this beach at Sewerby, just south of Flamborough Head in Yorkshire. It may be mentioned here that in the Gower Peninsula there are traces of one or two later

* *Proc. Geol. Assoc.*, 4, 1932, 291.

beaches, and that in Sussex, at Slindon, Goodwood, and elsewhere there are beaches at higher levels, and probably earlier than the *Patella* beach. The paucity of remains make any general correlation impossible. Before ending this section, however, it should be noted that the height of the *Patella* beach falls northwards.

In order of time the next beach we find in Britain is the badly named 100-ft beach of the west of Scotland. Traces of this have been known for many years, and Wright again was the first to put it in a proper sequence. But here we begin to meet serious difficulties. First of all it seems to be excluded from the upper water of certain sea-lochs, and the view is held that at that time the lochs were occupied by ice, and so the beach could not be formed in them. This is entirely consonant with the facts that off shore, in deeper water, clays, containing an Arctic fauna, were deposited. The correlation of the two phenomena leaves no doubt that the beach was of late-Glacial age, an age corresponding with the so-called Moraine glaciation of Scotland, which is now broken down into somewhat

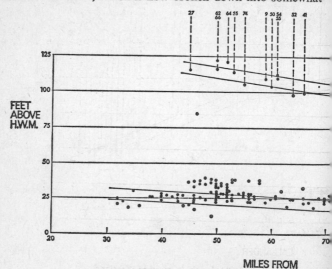

Fig. 16. *The tilting of the late-Glacial ('100-ft') beach*

smaller parts. The beach occurs at many places on the west coast, but is in no sense continuous. Moreover it is by no means everywhere of the same height, and certain features that have been regarded as beaches in the past are glacial outwash fans. Wright appreciated that the lower 25-ft beach was not everywhere at the same level, and he was not convinced that beaches at intermediate levels represented a separate distinct shoreline at about 50 ft. Donner, who based his evidence on good, but far too few, height measurements, concluded that there were four beaches – at 100, 50, 25, and 12 ft – all of which were horizontal. McCann measured heights at 191 sites, and from these he was able to show that there were in fact two beaches, a late-Glacial which varied in height from about 120 ft to rather less than 40 ft, and a post-Glacial beach the level of which varied between about 40 ft and rather less than 10 ft. The heights of both decrease from Callander, the higher one at 0·5 ft/mile, but at a distance of about 95 miles from that place the tilt increases to about 1·5

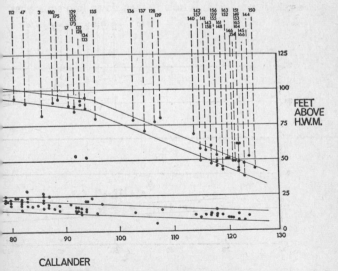

CALLANDER

*he post-Glacial ('25-ft') beach in western Scotland.*
*(By permission of Dr Brian McCann.)*

ft/mile. The lower declines in level at different rates in different directions, and the tilt is always much less than that of the higher beach (see Fig. 16).

The higher (former 100-ft) beach is nearly always cut in glacial drift. It is seldom continuous, and occurs in patches. Many terraces corresponding to this beach are deltaic in nature, including (McCann) the Ullapool delta; others are made of glacial outwash material. The often cited case of the gravel embankments at the entrance of Loch Carron near Strome Ferry do not reach the 130-ft level claimed by Wright, and the form and height of the gravel terraces along the Narrows emphatically suggest a marine origin, and that they belong to the late-Glacial sea. The gravels, however, are not of stream origin, but consist of glacial outwash re-worked by the sea. Along parts of the Applecross peninsula there is an erosion terrace cut in boulder clay; these terraces are somewhat lower (10–15 ft) than those at Loch Carron. There are similar terraces in the Firth of Lorne and Loch Linnhe, and those at Corran have been shown by McCann to be of fluvio-glacial origin; in fact, ice in the loch prevented the formation of a true late-Glacial raised beach.

These terraces must not be confused with the remarkable platform so well developed in north-east Islay, and also in Jura and Colonsay. The platform in Islay is broad, and backed by high cliffs; in Jura there are not any old cliffs behind the platform but locally there are great shingle spreads reaching up to 120 ft. In both islands the much later post-Glacial (= 25-ft) beach and shingle occur in front of the high platform. The high platform is pre-glacial in the sense that glacial deposits are found on it, but it is not yet possible to say whether it is pre- or inter-glacial in age. It is not known how it relates to the *Patella* beach of the south of England.

At a few feet above sea-level there is along much of the coast of Scotland a fine and well-developed bench on which rest gravels of the lower (25-ft) beach. Bench and gravels have usually been taken together and called the post-Glacial (25-ft) beach. But, as has been noted above, the level of the bench is not the same everywhere; it is tilted. Moreover, it does not follow that even if the gravels on it are post-glacial, the bench is also of the same date. The bench is often followed by the coast road in Wigtownshire, Ayrshire, and the west side of the Kintyre peninsula, and elsewhere. It is beautifully developed nearly all round Arran and the Cumbraes, and it is found in even more enclosed waters as in the channel between Luing and Seil and the mainland. There are many examples also on the east coast. It is noteworthy that there seems to be no lower bench corresponding to present sea-level, and this serves to emphasise an important point: under what circumstances was the bench cut? Even with a sea-level some 20–30 ft above the present, it is more than difficult to see how the bench could have been cut in the many narrow straits and firths where it is found. Moreover, it implies a long period of cutting, and there is now an increasing acceptance of the view that the bench is much older than the beach with which it is often associated. Anyone who travels around the coast of Scotland will find much to think about if he considers the origin and evolution of this bench. It is certainly being eroded and lowered today, and in some places might be considered as having been formed under present conditions.

There was, however, a considerable period of time separating the late-Glacial (100-ft) and post-Glacial (25-ft) beaches. This was marked by a low sea-level during which the submerged peat beds and forests were formed. It was Jamieson's classic paper on the deposits at the mouth of the Ythan in Aberdeenshire which established this sequence, and incidentally implied the idea of isostasy, although he did not use that word. Around many parts of our coast peat beds are often exposed at low water, and excavations for docks at Hull, Barry, and many other places have established the fact that the exposed beds are but the top of a series which is now hidden. Moreover, dredgings from the North Sea show that such beds exist on the Dogger Bank. These beds and buried river channels show clearly that after the late-Glacial (100-ft) episode, sea-level began to fall until it was about 200 ft or more below the present. The remains found in the submerged peat beds show that the climate improved a great deal, but it is still quite uncertain why the sea-level fell so as to expose much of the North Sea floor, and also the floors of shallow seas and inlets on the west coast of Britain. If we are right in thinking that a fall of sea-level is caused by an increase in glaciation, we must consider the suggestion put forward many years ago by W. B. Wright, that the fall in sea-level in our latitudes may have been caused by a recrudescence of the ice in the southern hemisphere. There is no doubt that the sequence of events in the British Isles was a fall in sea-level from about 100 ft in late-Glacial times to perhaps 200 ft below the present. This was followed by a rise of sea-level during which the peat beds were formed, and this rise continued until the sea was about 25 ft above the present level. This is shown not only by the raised beach deposits, but also, as Jamieson proved, by offshore clays. The beach deposits are now not all at the same level owing to tilting, a process which was probably in action during their formation as well as subsequent to it. Later the sea fell to its present level, but again because of differential movements, deposits associated with the fall are not everywhere at the same height relative to Ordnance Datum.

The events in late-Glacial times have been investigated in much detail by J. B. Sissons and others in eastern Scotland, and they have shown that there is in fact a large number of late-Glacial shorelines associated in part with advances and retreats of the ice. This work is based on most careful observations, the study of more than 2000 borehole records, and of more than 700 boreholes made by Sissons and his co-workers. The work has shown that there are several buried raised beaches, i.e. beaches in all respects like the visible ones, but now covered by deposits of a later transgression in the carse-lands of the Firth of Forth. Since we are concerned mainly with the way in which raised beaches and related phenomena affect the appearance of the coast, there is no need to enter into great detail. It will suffice to quote from Sissons (*Trans. Inst. Brit Geogrs.*, No. 28), who discusses sea-level changes in the Carse of Stirling: 'A glacial readvance about 10,300 years ago resulted in the formation of the Menteith moraine. Meltwaters cut breaches in the moraine and deposited outwash plains in

front of it. The main phase of outwash deposition appears to
have been related to a sea-level not exceeding 33 to 38 ft O.D.,
in the area immediately east of the moraine. Before the ice had
withdrawn from the moraine sea-level rose to 39–40 ft and
thereafter fell below 35 ft. A later marine transgression (to an
altitude of 34 to 36 ft in the area immediately east of the
moraine) probably culminated about 9500 years ago. A
relative fall of sea-level followed and was succeeded by a
still-stand, or more probably a slight transgression that probably terminated about 8800 years ago. Thereafter sea-level fell
again relative to the land, the minimal sea-level probably
occurring about 8500 years ago. Subsequently there was a
major rise of sea-level, initially rapid, that appears to have
culminated about 5500 years ago.'

It should not be thought that these movement have ceased.
There is ample evidence to show that up or down movements
of coastlines relative to sea-level are still in progress. Indeed it
would be unreasonable to assume that they have stopped. We
know that the Ice Age was punctuated by long intervals during
which the climate ameliorated; we do not know if we are now
living in one of them or in a truly post-glacial period. In
recent decades there are many authentic records of melting of
the ice in Arctic regions and of the retreat of glaciers in
temperate lands. This implies that sea-level must be rising. But
the increase in level from this reason alone is small, and is
probably to be measured in centimetres in a century. On the
other hand the isostatic movements of the land in its recovery
from the former great ice caps are still in progress. It is known
that Scandinavia is rising, and if the recent and post-glacial
shorelines of that area are mapped, they show that the land as
a whole is rising in the form of a very flat dome.

In the British Isles there is some evidence of a tilting movement. A broad ill-defined hinge runs across northern England.
The south-east of the country is sinking, the northern parts are
rising. We have not detailed evidence at many places, but tidal
records at Newlyn (near Penzance), Felixstowe and Dunbar
are most informative, and suggest a slight rise of sea-level at
each place. These tidal measurements began in 1918 and end-

ed, at Dunbar, in 1950 as a result of silting. The figures for Newlyn and Felixstowe are in close agreement; those for Dunbar are somewhat anomalous relative to the other stations. This rise of sea-level as indicated by tide-gauge records is unequivocal and is undoubtedly a combination of eustatic and isostatic processes. What is much more difficult to assess on any quantitative basis is the tilting, the isostatic, movement. There have been three comprehensive geodetic levellings of this country, and at first sight it would seem that the differences found in the height of any station between any two of these levellings implies a vertical movement, up or down, of that station. Unfortunately this is not wholly true. It is perhaps as well that this is so, since the figures suggest a lowering of south-east England of 1½ to 2 feet between 1850 and 1930! Despite the care and refinements taken with the levellings it seems that there is some systematic but not fully understood error in the precision levelling. It has been suggested 'that the direction of illumination of the (levelling) staff might affect the readings and that the tendency of the northerly staff to be illuminated by direct sunlight more frequently than the southerly staff might introduce systematic error into lines running generally north and south' (Major J. Kelsey, Commonwealth Survey Officers Conference, Cambridge, 1959).

Whatever the cause, there are, nevertheless, several considerations which show that the tilt referred to above is a fact. Along the Thames estuary there are numerous clear indications that the land has sunk relative to sea-level since Roman times. Then parts of central London were aits or eyots similar to Eel Pie or Chiswick Eyots today and Roman remains are now frequent below high tide and marsh level. In Roman times the tide limit in the Thames was approximately at London Bridge, now it is at Teddington. The great walls enclosing the Lower Thames are mediaeval in origin, and have been raised from time to time. At Brentford, Hallstadt pottery and Bronze Age implements have been found below the Roman level, and similar finds have been made near Southend and other places. There is no doubt that since Roman times the land around the estuary has sunk 15 ft or more, and the finding of earlier remains at lower levels implies that this movement has been going on for a much longer period. The same is true of the Low Countries.

But farther north in Great Britain, and also in north Denmark and Scandinavia, the reverse is the case. Recent work on Walney Island (J. L. Melville, *Barrow Nats. Field Club and Photo Soc.*, 1956, **8**, 25) suggests that in Roman-British times the island was six to eight feet lower relative to sea-level than it now is. The nature and distribution of the raised beaches and carselands of the Solway and farther north all bear this out. The sequence of deposits in the East Anglian and Humber fenlands have been studied in much detail. In both the order of events is similar but in the East Anglian area the corresponding features are at a somewhat lower level, again suggesting a tilt, and that the Humber was near to the hinge line. We need to know much more of this problem which in the course of one or two centuries may have serious consequences on harbour and dock installations. In general the movement is in the nature of a tilt, but in 1950 excavations made for a power station at Great Yarmouth afforded evidence of a post-Saxon movement. Whether this was a purely local movement is not yet certain, but it undoubtedly makes the problem more complex.

The serious coastal flooding resulting from the storm surge in 1953 led to the appointment of a departmental committee under the Chairmanship of Lord Waverley. Among many other matters the sea defences in the Thames were considered at length, and important tests were carried out on the tidal model of the river belonging to the Port of London Authority. Various suggestions were made and emphasis was given to the notion of interposing 'a suitable structure across the portion of the river between Purfleet and Greenhithe known as Long Reach. This structure would be provided with "gates" so as to leave the waterway clear except on the rare occasions of impending high flood when it [would become] necessary to operate the "gates".

'This is clearly a most interesting possibility, but one which involves formidable engineering and financial consideration, and we do not think we can do more than set out the technical problem together with this suggestion which has been made to us for a solution. We think it important, however, that this suggestion should be investigated and a decision reached as quickly as possible, since the decision as to basic methods of protection will necessarily govern the executive works to be undertaken by the responsible authorities.'

The continued sinking of south-eastern England, and the possibility of another storm surge make this a matter of serious import. It is more than worth while to consider what the Dutch have already accomplished in the Delta Plan (see p. 123). For various reasons their coast is more vulnerable than ours, but a possible threat to the Thames estuary cannot be overlooked, and for reasons outlined in this chapter is likely to become of increasing significance in the future.

# 6. Coral Coasts

In this chapter the main emphasis will be given to the coasts and islands associated with coral reefs. But a brief introduction to the origin of coral reefs may be helpful. About the middle of last century the work of Darwin and Dana emphasised for the first time the great problems associated with reefs. Both men held similar views, and the division of reefs into Fringing, Barrier, and Atoll reefs is as acceptable now as it was then. But this does not automatically imply the acceptance of Darwin's view that a fringing reef having first formed around an island or along a mainland coast would be converted into a barrier reef by the sinking of the land, and that an atoll reef is the product of a fringing reef that originated around an island or volcanic cone which finally sank below sea-level. On the other hand no one would deny that profound submergence has taken place in some places, and consequently some atolls may well have been formed as Darwin suggested.

Darwin's subsidence hypothesis was a magnificent generalisation, but inevitably it soon met with criticism. Why should such subsidence have taken place? Why should it have been so widespread? These and other questions were unanswerable, and so it is not surprising that a number of scientists, including Murray, Semper, Agassiz and others put forward alternative views which did not involve major vertical measurements. There is no need to discuss these views in detail; they usually implied the presence of a platform on which corals could build. The coral polyp is exacting in its needs. Its lower limit of growth is probably mainly determined by the penetration of light, and is not likely to be more than 40–50 fathoms. It requires a water temperature of approximately 70°F, and it thrives best in clear water. These factors limit its growth mainly

to tropical regions, and because of the cooler water on the
western sides of continents (e.g. the Humboldt Current and up-
welling along the west South American coast) the main reef
areas are on the east of the continental land masses, but reefs
may, or course, encircle large islands, e.g. New Caledonia. But
the opponents of Darwin and Dana ran into a difficulty. Why
should so many platforms at the right, or approximately right,
depth for coral growth have been present? Moreover, if the
platforms were cut this must also imply the cutting of cliffs
behind them. It was also suggested that in many places where
either platforms or submarine features were too far below the
surface that they had been built up to the required level by the
deposition of deep sea oozes. There is no doubt that oozes are
deposited on such places, but their accumulation is extremely
slow, and even if it were rapid, it is impossible to think of these
forming a table-shaped mass on a small submarine feature; they
would have slipped down into deeper water.

The divergence of views led to the suggestion that if a bore
were put down in a suitably chosen atoll reef it would show
that either subsidence had taken place or that the reef was
built on a platform or relatively shallow depth. In 1912 the
Royal Society sponsored an expedition to the atoll of Funa-
futi in the Gilbert and Ellice Islands. A bore was put down to
1114 ft, and the cores were carefully analysed. The upper part
of the bore passed through coral *in situ*, but a great deal of the
remainder was pulverised, and although coral masses were
traversed it was contended by the opponents of subsidence
that there was no clear proof that the coral was *in situ*, and
that the probability was that the bore cut through a talus on
the edge of the reef. Dr Hinde, who was in charge of the
investigation, argued that the balance of evidence was in
favour of subsidence, but nevertheless the general opinion
seemed to be that although subsidence was indicated, the
evidence was not entirely convincing. In 1952 the evidence
was reviewed by Dr T. F. Grimsdale who thought that at least
the lower half of the core indicated that coral growth was able
to keep pace with the rise of sea-level. Later, talus accumulated
during a more rapid rise of the sea to be followed by a time

when the reef grew outwards once again. (*Occasional Papers*, Challenger Society, 1952.)

In 1915 a major advance was made by Daly. He had been in the Hawaiian Islands and had found traces of glaciation on some of the highest peaks. He noticed, too, that the reefs did not cover all the area of the platforms. This led him to suggest that in the Ice Age the sea temperatures in places some distance from the Equator (Honolulu is in lat. 21°N.) would have been reduced below that at which coral could thrive. Moreover, not only would the temperature of the water have fallen, but so also would the level of the oceans because the only way in which the great ice-caps could have accumulated would have been by moisture derived from the oceans. Calculations of the extent and volume of the ice-caps led Daly to suggest a lowering of 200–300 ft. There is no doubt that a change of level of this order took place, and modern work in this respect has done little more than modify Daly's estimate. A change of this sort means that at the time of low sea-level the reefs previously existing in places where the water temperature also fell, could have been killed and destroyed. In such places, and also on islands and coasts the world over, the sea could begin to cut platforms at levels accordant with the change. Only in the warmest parts of the globe could coral continue to thrive, and even there, as a result of the fall in sea-level, the parts of the reef exposed would have been destroyed, but since coral growth was maintained at the new sea-level neither platforms nor cliffs could have been cut. In so far as the marginal areas of coral growth were concerned, and also in the non-coral areas, platforms might have been formed on which reefs could have grown on the return of favourable temperature conditions and the rise of sea-level. These reefs could enclose lagoons of roughly accordant depths, depths that would agree within small limits with conditions suitable for coral growth, and agreeable to the views of Murray and others who opposed subsidence. It will be appreciated, however, that in the places where coral did not cease to grow, the evidence of platform depth is conflicting.

This was a great step forward, but in its simple form the

theory gave too many platforms! But (see p. 82) the growth of
the ice-caps not only caused changes in sea-level, but also, by
their weight, set up isostatic readjustment in the land masses.
These movements are still in progress, and one result is that in
the glaciated areas platforms may not have been cut if the ice
advanced over the coast, but even where they were cut, they
could now be, as a result of land uplift, at considerably higher
levels. Apart, however, from the platforms and consequent
cliffs, no discussion had taken place concerning the nature of
the coasts within the reefs, nor, with one or two exceptions, of
the coral islands themselves. It was left to W. M. Davis to
show how the physiography of the coasts might help in the
problem. His approach was somewhat academic, but he
enlarged on the nature of cliffs within reefs, and he pointed out
that if it could be shown that valleys were drowned to depths
considerably greater than the assumed fall in sea-level, then
there was strong argument for subsidence. Daly's theory
implied drowned valleys to about 300 ft; but cases are known
of valleys submerged to much greater depths, even if now they
are partially filled with recent sediments.

In late years much has been learned about coral reefs by
bores and still more by seismic methods. Both have shown that
the problem of origin is more complex than can be comprised
by any one theory. Bores on the Great Barrier Reefs of
Australia showed, even at relatively small depths, that the
coral rested on sediments, often siliceous in origin. The bores
did not reach solid rock. On Bikini Atoll more than 2000 ft,
mainly, of sediment – not ooze – were found under the coral,
and it is extremely difficult to see how it could have accumulated. In short, there is no one simple answer. In some places
subsidence has undoubtedly taken place; elsewhere coasts have
been stable or perhaps built up by sediment to the level at
which corals can begin to grow. This, after all, is what might
have been expected, and it emphasises the need for careful
investigation of all reef areas.

The nature of the coast within a barrier reef will depend to
some extent upon whether the reef was destroyed in the ice age.
If it were, then one may expect to find cliffs, probably now

largely or wholly submerged by the subsequent rise of sea-level. The tops of high cliffs may still rise above sea-level, but clearly a careful bathymetric survey is required. In places where coral continued to grow, the coast within the reef may or may not be cliffed; much will depend upon the width of the lagoon and the nature of the rocks and local factors. The point can be illustrated very well on the Queensland coast. Although coral reefs extent from Torres Strait to about the latitude of Rockhampton, it is only north of Trinity Opening (north-east of Cairns) that the reef forms a true barrier. In this part and probably a little farther south, it probably existed in the Ice Age, and it is also in this area that it is much closer to the coast. But the enclosed sea is several miles wide, ranging from six or seven miles at Cape Melville to 80 miles or more in the far north, and the Trade Winds give rise to effective wave action within it. Hence, the coast is locally cliffed, but only to a minor degree, and in more sheltered parts scarcely at all. On the other hand, south of Cairns the degree of cliffing is much greater since the reefs are a long way from the coast and the fetch of the waves is more extensive. In the southern parts it is probable that reef growth ceased in the Ice Age and so the coast shows normal cliffing. Comparable features, allowing for local conditions, are found in other barriers, e.g. New Caledonia, but the scale of conditions on the Queensland coast is not reached elsewhere.

Coral islands, in the popular sense, may mean islands of solid rock and carrying perhaps a dense and varied vegetation area, or merely simple sand islands built by wave action on a reef. The former are in general similar to a mainland coast bordered by a reef; they will show cliffs and valleys and associated features consonant with the size and shape of the island and lagoon. It is with the second type that we are mainly concerned. All these purely reef islands are wave built, but may be increased somewhat in height and area by the interaction of sand accumulation and plant growth. The simplest type is the sand-cay. These originate as flat heaps of sand produced by the wear and tear of wave action on a reef. If they stand on isolated reefs they are likely to be on the lee side, and it is often possible when on such a cay, to see the waves approaching from windward and curling round the reef and washing up behind the cay. If some such mechanism is not present the sand is likely to be washed completely off the reef. Cays and even more complicated structures of similar nature, may be completely destroyed in a storm of hurricane. If, however, a cay attains a reasonable degree of stability, it is only a matter of time before seeds of plants reach it, and a carpet of vegetation begins to form. At first plants such as *Sesuvium* and *Ipomea pes-caprae* come in; later they may be followed by shrubs and, in many parts of the Pacific, the coconut palm may appear by natural means.

But such small and isolated islands are often too ephemeral for a dense plant cover or large trees to grow. If there are bigger reefs, true atolls, a similar process goes on but along greater lengths of reef. Moreover, large lumps of coral may be cast up on the reef in storms, and these may perhaps form the nuclei of sand islands. If we picture an extensive atoll reef, it is probable that the process of island formation on it will begin on its windward side. The reef is likely to be broken by channels leading to the lagoon, and so instead of one long island developing, several smaller ones may form. But in all, the process of building is similar to that of the cay. The waves pulverise the reef and form sand which is in part washed across the surface of the reef. Some of it may begin to gather round coral boulders, but this, although common, is not a necessity. If the winds are variable islands may form on any part of the reef, and the lagoon may be not only reef-enclosed, but island-enclosed as well. Just as on a simple cay, vegetation begins to grow, and it is only a matter of time before the coral-island-lagoon system is built up. These islands are never more than a few feet high; locally the sand may be piled a little higher, but in hurricane areas they are liable to be overwashed, or even destroyed.

There are many variations of this pattern. Umbgrove, and Kuenen of the Snellius expedition, described those in the Bay of Djakarta. Within the northern part of the Australian Barrier Reefs there are numerous islands built on isolated patch reefs within the steamer channel, i.e. they are quite separate

from the outer barrier. Some of these consist of a single cay,
nearly always situated on or near the lee (north-west) side of
the reef, and a series of ridges of coral shingle, enclosing a
mangrove swamp, on the weather side. The two parts of the
island are often distinct, and separated by the reef flat, *not* by
a lagoon. Sometimes the two parts are telescoped so that the
shingle ridges enclose or are wrapped round the cay. In these
cases the shingle area is usually smaller, and the sand cay with
its dry land vegetations stands out in marked contrast to the
dark green of the mangroves. Other minor variations occur;
the shingle-mangrove area may be fairly well developed, but the
cay may be but a sandbank awash at high water. Nevertheless
the relative positions of the two are similar. In one instance, at
least, the shingle mangrove island was on one reef, and the cay
on another close to it.

On all these islands, and on many parts of mainland and
island beaches in the Tropics, beach rock or beach conglomerate
is found. These are similar in origin; the difference is in the
size of the material cemented. There is still much to be learnt
about the formation of beach rock. I have studied it both in
the Queensland coastal area and in the cays around Jamaica.
That the sands or pebbles are cemented by carbonate of lime is
clear; what is by no means easy to explain is the distribution of
the patches of rock. In those cases I know it had formed
between the tide marks, or possibly in the rather wider zone in
which there is a good deal of spray. In appearance a typical
beach-rock is slab-like, the slabs dipping at the angle of slope
of the beach. There may be several layers. In Queensland
waters the beach rock was best developed on the windward side
of the sand cays. I saw no island completely surrounded by it.
This was also true of the Jamaican cays, but there the tidal
range is very small, less than one foot. The rock may owe its
position to drainage of water from the cay, but this does not
seem to explain its mainly windward position. The shingle
ridges of the mangrove area are often similarly cemented, and
if, as is sometimes the case, the original bedding of the
shingle dipped seawards, then the exposed and worn upper
edges form an exceedingly rough pavement.

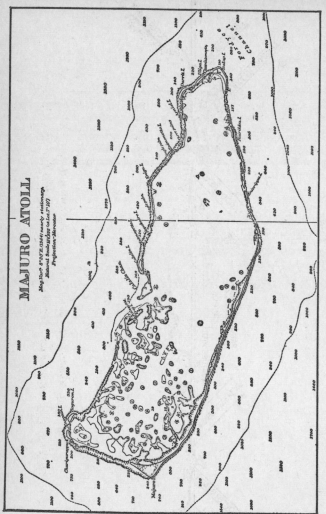

Fig. 17 (a).

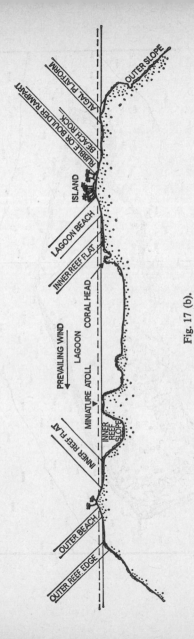

Fig. 17 (a). *Majuro Atoll. (Based on the U.S. Government chart of 1944.)*

Fig. 17 (b). *Section across a coral reef to show main features. (After Eibl-Eibesfeldt, 1964.)*

Fig. 17 (b).

Whatever the true origin of the rock may be, it undoubtedly has significant physiographical effects. It makes a hard and resistant skin to the cays, and in storms pieces are broken off and washed up to the beach crest, often giving a line or zone of coarse boulders. Moreover, many examples in Queensland and Jamaica showed that on occasions the cay may be wholly or partially washed out from within the beach rock which is left standing as isolated rocky ridges. Changes in the form of cay produced by storms can often be seen by the varying trends of lines of beach-rock around it. This cementation process can also take place on parts of a mainland coast. If it does it certainly helps as a defence work.

Since beach rock is formed more or less within the tidal range, or spray zone, it follows that if it is found at higher or lower levels there has probably been some sort of vertical movement since its formation. In Queensland there were numerous examples of beach rock, or beach conglomerate, well above the present limit of high water. Moreover, these outcrops were often much weathered, and considerably different in appearance from that now forming. They also corresponded in level to features, such as wave-cut benches, on the coast of rocky islands or of the mainland. In the Morant cays, about 60 miles south-east of Jamaica there were several traces of beach rock below the level of that now forming. The various levels in Queensland seemed to be consistent, and suggested a sea-level (eustatic) movement, but the submerged beach rock in the Morant cays may well only indicate some local movement.

Important work on the cays off the coast of British Honduras has been completed by D. R. Stoddart. In addition to commenting on beach rock, he draws attention to cay sandstone, which has been described by other writers. Cay sandstone implies cementation of sands above sea-level. It often has a nearly horizontal surface but may be inclined with the surface on which it forms. Stoddart suggests that it may be associated with the percolation of rain water to the water table and he states that it was not seen on any cay that did not possess a known lens of fresh water. It is exposed when cover-

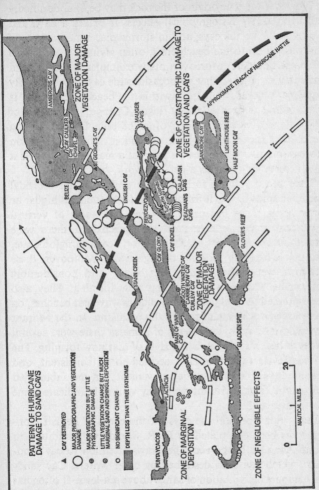

Fig. 18. The Belize hurricane, 1961. (D. R. Stoddart.)

ing sand is removed and in certain circumstances may resemble raised beach rock, and therefore give a false impression of uplift.

Stoddart was particularly fortunate in being able to visit and map the Honduras cays both shortly before and very soon after Hurricane Hattie swept the area in October 1961. The cays are in general similar to those described already, but there are many variations in detail and size depending much upon the slopes and areas of the reefs and local conditions. In the main track of the hurricane wind speeds reached 150 miles/h, and sea-level rose as much as 15 ft, and severe wave action was superimposed on this. Consequently, the damage was greatest in the central belt and diminished outwards so that Stoddart was able to recognise three distinct zones (see Fig. 18). In the central zone some cays were swept away and damage was catastrophic. No instance was found where beach rock stopped shore retreat, but it was noticeable that 'well developed and undisturbed natural vegetation appeared much more effective in cay preservation'.

This does not necessarily contradict the statement made earlier that beach rock may act as a protection; much must depend on local conditions, length of outcrops, wave and wind incidence and other factors. Stoddart's summary of the effect of the hurricane on vegetation is interesting: 'the most striking vegetational changes . . . were the widespread defoliation of *Rhizophora* and other mangroves; and the destruction of beach and marginal vegetation, often through movement of the substrate, involving the complete disappearance over a 30-mile wide area of such characteristic cay species as *Tournefortia gnaphalodes* and *Suriana maritima*'. Study of the map (Fig. 18) will explain the distribution and degree of damage in the five zones (i.e. the central belt plus two of decreasing damage on either side of it) in relation to the path of the hurricane and the natural features over which it passed. (See *Atoll Research Bulletin*, No. 5, 1963. The Pacific Science Board, National Academy of Sciences, U.S.A. This was the first time that detailed surveys of cays had been made before and after a hurricane.)

# 7. Sea Defences

Anyone who has seen even a limited amount of the south and east coast of England will realise something of the great problem of defending the land from the attack of the sea. He will also realise that in some places accretion is going on and that locally the land is gaining. If we consider the whole coast of Great Britain we can still fully agree with the findings of the Royal Commission of 1911, that *in toto*, the amount gained by natural and artificial reclamation exceeds that lost by erosion. But accretion is to most people a slow and unspectacular process, whereas the washing away of a cliff and the possible collapse of buildings on its edge is news. Erosion, since man has increasingly made use of the coast, has become of ever greater significance. Moreover, the constant loss of land, some of it of agricultural value, is a serious matter.

The natural defence against erosion is a good beach. The waves expend their energy on this and the land within is safe. But what is a good beach? The constant wear and tear of erosion means that any beach must sooner or later cease to be of use in this respect unless it is constantly replenished with new material. The matter is, of course, complicated, but how it works in practice may partly be illustrated by the Lincolnshire coast in the great storm of 1953. Between Mablethorpe and Skegness, although the beach appeared wide, erosion had been active in ordinary storms and every now and again the surface sand was removed and exposed the eroded clays below. But the southerly drift of beach material has led to progradation and accretion south of Skegness, and to the north of Mablethorpe the beach and sandy marsh areas are very wide. Hence, in the 1953 storm severe damage took place between the two towns, whereas to the north of Mablethorpe and to the south of Skegness, although some dunes were eroded and some flooding took place on account of the abnormally high level of the water and unusual wave action, the erosion and loss were negligible. This is an extreme instance, but on any coast faced for some distance by sandy beaches the same kind of phenomena may be observed.

It is with this in view that groynes and breakwaters are built. As shown in Chapter 2 material travels along an open coast, and if its lateral displacement can be halted, then it will pile up at that place. How much will accumulate will depend primarily on the amount in transit and also on the length and height of the groynes. It will also depend on whether the groynes are solid structures or permeable in the sense that some material may pass through them. If we, for the moment, just think of one groyne, we shall note that while material piles up on one side, on the other scour is likely to take place and the beach level may fall. It is, therefore, at once apparent that great care must be taken in the height, length, spacing, and siting of groynes. Since most groynes can, if necessary, be raised in height, it is usually far better to start with low ones so that the up-drift side does not rise too much in level relative to the down-drift side. The spacing also matters. The object is usually to raise the general level of a beach, and so each individual groyne should act in this way, and not in such a way as to obstruct the one next down-drift. For this same reason the height of the groynes above the normal beach level should only be such as to cause a reasonable amount of accumulation, and allow surplus sand to pass over, through, or round each groyne. Occasionally it may be thought necessary to build much higher groynes, and so cause great irregularities in the height of the beach. This is particularly well illustrated at Eastbourne.

Permeable groynes and chain groynes allow some material to pass through or over them, and undoubtedly in some places they are of considerable value. They are apt to be somewhat unsightly, and are seldom used along a promenade or sea front. But groynes of any sort, although they may well have a

beneficial effect at the place where they are built, by no means
necessarily have such a good effect on the coast down-drift of
them. If they succeed in holding up all or most of the drift, it
follows that the coast to leeward is deprived of that material,
and so is likely to suffer erosion. In the past it was only too
common for groynes to have this effect, and the evil is by no
means completely eliminated.

A coastal resort naturally wishes to have a good beach, and
to do so often has recourse to building groynes. In the past this
has frequently been done in such a way as to deprive the coast
down-drift of the normal supplies, and so cause erosion. The
matter can be more serious if harbour works intensify the
effect. There are many examples of this and Great Yarmouth
illustrates it well. The drift along the east Norfolk and
Suffolk coasts is to the south. The joint mouth of the Yare,
Bure and Waveney is deflected by the spit on which Yarmouth
stands, and the harbour mouth is between two piers which act
as long and high groynes. As a consequence, the beach forming Yarmouth denes continues to accumulate, whereas at
Gorleston just south of the harbour there is erosion, recently
held by the building of sea walls. The same kind of process is
happening at Lowestoft and Southwold, and at Shoreham and
other places on the south coast. It is difficult to see an overall
remedy for this state of affairs. A harbour like that at Great
Yarmouth must function and it can only do so with the help of
the present harbour works. In theory it may seem easy to
devise a plan that would balance loss and gain along a long
stretch of coast, but in practice it is almost impossible. If we
could start afresh and rebuild our towns and harbours something might be done, but that is out of the question. The problem is an inherited one, and goes right back to the original
sitings of our coastal towns. A very striking instance is seen on
the Holderness coast (see p. 80). The whole of that coast is
subject to severe erosion, and the two small towns of Hornsea
and Withernsea have had to be defended by seawalls. As a
consequence these two defended areas are beginning to become
salients, a process that is likely to become more pronounced
as time goes on.

The east coast of Florida is low and sandy, and along it there are many well-known resorts, including Palm Beach and Miami. At Miami there are numerous groynes, both of wood and steel, but there is but little beach. It has been estimated that about 85 per cent of the visitors seldom, if ever, use the beach, but instead swim in the many bathing pools which have been built inside it. The beach itself is somewhat steep, and there are dangerous currents, and a great deal of shell sand. In short, there is no adequate source of material to feed the beach. Some miles to the north of Miami is Palm Beach. Here there is an inlet, and jetties have been built so that the northern jetty holds up the southerly directed flow. As a consequence (cf. Yarmouth) the coast to the south has suffered, but the trouble has to some extent been overcome by means of a by-passing sand-plant which is capable of passing up to a quarter of a million cubic yards of sand across the inlet every year. Further replenishment is made by means of dredging sand from deeper water. Sand-passing plants of this sort are not uncommon. All inlets are likely to present problems if they have to be used for navigation purposes; those through sandy beaches are often the most troublesome.

Before building groynes or building jetties alongside the outlets of rivers or tidal creeks, it is important to learn as much as possible about the action of waves and currents on the coast. In the past, defences have all too often been erected on far too little evidence. Local people interested in a particular piece of coast can often give much useful information and, if their observations cover several years, they may be able to put the effect of damaging storms into a proper perspective. On the other hand their observations cannot be in any true sense quantitative. Reference to Chapter 2 will explain how radio-active and other tracers can be used on a length of coast so as to enable the engineer to obtain a far more precise estimate of the volume and nature of the littoral drift. What is more, it is common practice in a hydrological laboratory to make a model of a piece of coast so that the effects of winds and waves from different directions can be studied. Miniature groynes can be erected on the model, and careful observation will indicate how they should be spaced, and how long they should be to give the best results.

Tidal range has not yet been specifically mentioned in this chapter. Littoral drift (see Chapter 2) takes place in tidal as well as tideless seas. In the former, especially if there is shingle on the beaches, the effects of drift are often more noticeable on the higher parts of the beach. There are many places around our own coasts which show shingle collected between groynes on the upper part of the beach. In fact in some localities the shingle alone is worked on at high water and (see p. 16) there may be opposite movements of shingle and sand on the same beach. If the beach is composed wholly, or almost wholly, of sand the effect may be much the same whatever the range of the tide, but the consequences may be less noticeable.

Associated with groynes there may be, in fact there usually are, sea walls or promenades. The function of the groynes in such a place is to collect a beach in front of the wall. But the nature of the wall itself is important. This is in no sense a book concerned with the building and structure of sea walls, so details will only be given where relevant. But something must be said about the slope and face of sea walls. In the past many walls were built with a vertical or near vertical face. At high water waves break directly on such a wall, or may be reflected from it. The waves may sooner or later smash the wall, and in any case are liable to cause an increase of erosion and scour at its foot. Walls of this sort are sometimes strengthened with sheet piling or masonry aprons. These may have a beneficial effect, although it may not be long lasting. Many walls of this nature in northern Florida, near Jacksonville, have collapsed. If vertical walls are used in deeper water they may be very successful '. . . vertical walls may be used in depths of water sufficiently great to prevent the breaking of waves, and where the sea bed is resistant to erosion, provided that the foundations are not subject to irregular settlement. Where these two latter conditions are not present, vertical walls can still be employed provided that special measures are undertaken to counteract such conditions.' (H. F. Cornick, *Dock Harb. Engng.*, 1959, **2**, 118.)

Sloping walls, however, are by no means always more successful. They may vary somewhat in pattern; some are stepped, some straight, others may have a seaward directed cornice at the top, and there are many other variations in detail. The infilling of the walls will vary with circumstances, especially the availability of materials and expense. But whatever the filling may be, the seaward slope must be faced with some sort of watertight material. Frequently, the toe of the wall is strengthened by sheet piling. Sloping walls, many of which have to be filled with sand, clay, or shingle, are usually built on coasts where natural rock cannot be quarried within easy reach. Every wall is subject to special conditions peculiar to the locality in which it is built, but certain general points apply to all. Storm waves breaking on these walls cause an uprush of water, and the succeeding backwash flows quickly back, with little or no infiltration as on a normal beach, and so not only washes any loose material seawards but meets the next wave trough, but not so as to retard it. Thus the new wave advances, breaks somewhere near the toe of the wall and a great deal of turbulence is set up. This means nearly always not only that any loose material is taken from the face of the wall, but also that scour, often powerful, is set up and removes material from in front of the toe. Thus the beach slope is lowered, and unless conditions at some later stage bring in new sand or shingle, the whole beach becomes liable to increased erosion. The slope of these walls may be straight or curved, but the main advantages of either 'is the fact that they are better adapted for construction on beaches of poor foundation value, providing any detrimental influence from the land side is prevented, such as the seeping of water through the base engendering a quicksand effect'. Some sloping walls are stepped. Such a wall may well break up the upward swash and the backwash and thus render the destructive effect less. If the steps are high, their effect is almost that of a vertical wall. In a severe storm it may be found that there is serious scour at the toe of the wall, and sand and especially shingle may be piled up on the treads of the steps. Once again sheet piling may be necessary to protect the toe of the wall. There is, in fact, no fixed rule; some prefer to build vertical walls – and local circumstances may compel this – others to construct sloping walls. Much must depend on local conditions, finance, and sometimes on the appearance of the wall when finished.

The Advisory Committee on Sea Defence Research in 1960 put certain questions to the Director of the Hydraulics Station at Wallingford, England. These were answered in a short and interesting paper by R. C. H. Russell, who later became Director. One of these questions was 'How should the designer determine the profile of a wall, especially to avoid toe scour?' The answer was that walls with flatter slopes are better than those with steeper slopes for two reasons. Wave reflection is far less from flatter slopes. Reflected waves do not merely affect the immediate locality of the breaking waves, but cause turbulence for some distance seawards. This brings more material into suspension and thus allows currents to carry it away. Experiments have shown that if there are steps on the wall face they will reduce the height of the uprush, and will have little effect on reflection unless they are unusually high. On a very flat wall the waves break directly, and this may be important at high tide when erosion at the toe mainly occurs. The flatter the slope the more remote the sand at the toe is from the intense turbulence caused by the breaking wave. A slope of approximately 1 in 2 is the minimum condition for getting waves to break on the wall itself.

Apart from masonry and steel walls, many miles of coast, mainly in estuaries and sheltered waters, are protected by earth embankments. Between the Humber and Dover there are about 1200 miles of such banks. They are all built of local material which is usually dug from the adjacent marshes. The great surge of 1953 tested these walls severely, and caused many breaches in them. It also led to a considerable amount of research work, so that now we have much greater knowledge of how to build and maintain this type of wall than we had previously, but their maintenance in a high state of repair is expensive. Analysis of bank failures in 1953 revealed that on those banks facing more open water and consequently protected by some kind of facing, damage was relatively slight.

Even on an unfaced bank *direct* erosion seldom led to collapse. If waves splashed over or overtopped banks, surface scour on their inner side was often severe. However, the fundamental reason for failure was undoubtedly slipping or slumping of the inner face caused by seepage.

Because these banks are so often built of marsh clay, they are liable to shrinkage in drying, and so cracks develop. If then a storm raises the water level on a bank in this condition, much water may penetrate into the bank, and induce slips on the landward side and thus cause a lowering of the surface of the bank and so lead to a breach. This might well mean that failure could take place without any water passing over the bank before slumping had lowered the surface. If the inner parts of the bank are built mainly of sandy clay it may be pervious throughout. One particular bank, at Dartford Creek, collapsed in 1953 because it rested on a more permeable layer which the water penetrated and so lifted the whole bank. Some very interesting experiments were later made by the Building Research Station, and it is relevant to quote: 'A steel sheet-pile cofferdam was constructed on the river side of a 60-ft length of disused bank, and water was pumped into this cofferdam from a collecting basin dug on the landward side. A series of experiments were made in which typical tides were reproduced with peaks below the crest level of the bank. The quantity of water seeping through the bank, and the pore-water pressures developed in the body of the bank, were measured. Careful watch was kept for movement of the bank. Progressively higher tides were applied until the crest level was reached and finally water was allowed to trickle over the top of the bank. No movement was observed until this stage was reached and then a shallow slip suddenly occurred in the fissured clay on the backslope. This left a vertical face about $2\frac{1}{2}$ ft deep near the rear crest, and within a few moments the thin barrier of soil at the crest was quickly broken through, resulting in an initial breach, $2\frac{1}{2}$ ft deep at the centre, of the slipped section. This could have developed into a major breach had the water level been maintained. The test provided valuable confirmation of earlier predictions and also a starting

point on which to base further experiments to study improvement works.' (*Building Research*, D.S.I.R., 1956, **34**.)

This experiment once again shows how essential it is to
make use of models whenever possible before deciding on
some piece of coastal engineering. It cannot be too often
emphasised that however similar two or more pieces of coast
may appear, the conditions to which they are subjected are not
precisely the same. Hence the remedy applied to one place is
not necessarily that best adapted for anywhere else.

In broad terms the erection or maintenance of sea defence
works in England is primarily the concern of river boards and
local authorities under the surveillance of the Ministry of
Agriculture, Fisheries and Food for uncliffed coasts, and of
the Ministry of Housing and Local Government for cliffed
coasts. The Scottish and Welsh Offices deal with the matter in
those countries. A Government grant of 75 per cent – on
occasions more – is made to the authority concerned. In practice this system works very well, but it is not a national system
and there is no overall plan of coastal defence. At this stage in
the history of our coast any such plan is impracticable, but the
more the defence of any particular stretch of coast can be seen
as an item in that of the defence of the coast as a whole, so
much the better. It is still not unfair to say that sea defence is
thought of too much in terms of purely local conditions, and
that defence schemes are inevitably too much on an *ad hoc*
basis. The increasing use made of scale model experiments is
most certainly overcoming this, but there is still scope for much
fundamental research on coastal matters. Per Brunn, whose
work in Denmark and later in America, especially Florida, is
well known, emphasises this point and insists that we must do
our utmost to understand coastal phenomena in order to plan
ahead. 'Coastal research includes a great number of subjects
ranging from the implacement of huge breakwaters on the
ocean bottom for the purpose of checking ocean waves and
sand drift to the planting of proper vegetation in marsh areas
and on dunes for checking sediment transport by water on
sand. The employees involved in this research programme are
recruited from a great variety of fields in arts and sciences,

geology, geography, soil mechanics, coastal engineering, hydraulic engineering, oceanography, physics, mathematics and meteorology. In order that a coastal set-up shall be a complete and fully effective organisation it must include people from all these fields which in mutual good understanding "carry the ball" of coastal research.

'A discussion of the economic justification of such research requires a discussion of the applied sides of research aspects, but it should never be forgotten that without fundamental research applied research of any importance is impossible.' ('Coastal Research and its Economic Justification', in *Guide Book, Denmark*, International Geographical Congress, 1960.)

In the Netherlands sea defence is a national concern. That country suffered far more severely than Britain did in 1953, and sea defence schemes which had been carried out, or were in process, suddenly became of far greater significance, and were incorporated in what has become known throughout the world as the Delta Plan. Before discussing this it must be emphasised that throughout history Holland has had to take measures against the encroachment by the sea. The earliest structures were terpen or mounds in the marshes on which farms were built, and the building of sea and river walls. In a storm such as that of 1953 the winds, and consequently wave action, were directly onshore; on British coasts they were, except on the north-facing shores of the Moray Firth, Norfolk, and Kent, slightly offshore. Moreover, the whole coast of the Netherlands is low and the whole country has been slowly sinking relative to sea-level for a long period of time. The delta of the Rhine and Meuse and the numerous delta islands now embanked and in some cases joined together, have given to Holland a very irregular coast in the province of Zeeland, and a surge and severe onshore storm builds up the level of the water in the many channels between the islands, and so causes great and increasing pressure on the long lines of sea wall enclosing the islands and parts of the mainland. The maintenance of these banks is a difficult and costly process so that any practicable means of shortening the coast would not only lighten this particular problem – the existing banks would

become second lines of defence – but also for the same reason
would add to the safety of the country. It is not necessary here
to discuss in any detail the engineering problems involved in
dyke maintenance, but it is proper to call attention to what
happened all too frequently in and as a result of the 1953 storm.

The height reached by the water at that time was exceptional,
but since the surge did not coincide with a particularly high
spring tide, it must be conceded that a future surge could reach
some feet higher. Nevertheless in 1953 many sea walls in Holland were breached, and the lowlying land within flooded.
Largely because of the low levels of many of the flooded areas,
succeeding tides, once a breach had been made, flooded and
ebbed through the breaches, and by the scour so produced
deepened them, sometimes to more than 100 ft, and also
widened them. It was, therefore a major engineering operation to close many of these breaches. If this point is borne in
mind it is easy to understand that any effective shortening of
the whole coast is eminently desirable. Experience had already
been gained in this way earlier in this century. The great wall
enclosing the Zuider Zee was finally completed on 28 May
1932. This resulted in a large increase of the land area, and
also the replacement of a salt-water gulf by a fresh-water lake,
Lake Yssel. Moreover, it very greatly reduced the length of
vulnerable coastline. On a smaller scale the enclosure of the
Lauwerzee, a few miles to the east of the former Zuyder Zee, is
also to be undertaken. It is a much smaller project – 20 miles of
sea walls will be replaced by a dam 8 miles long – but it comes
within the general framework of the Delta Plan although it is
far away from Zeeland.

Fig. 19 shows the delta area in 1300 and 1950; and a com-
parison of the two maps is a sufficient comment on what the
Dutch have done to maintain their coast in six and a half
centuries. Fig. 20 shows the main outlines of the Delta Plan. It
will be seen that there are what may be called major and
(relatively) minor dams. The so-called three island scheme,
Walcheren and North and South Beveland, preceded the Delta
Plan, but was not undertaken before 1953 on account of expense. After the catastrophe of 1953, however, the whole

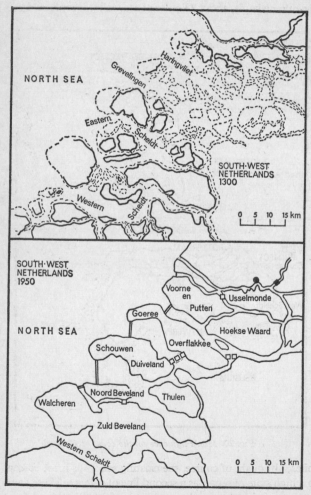

Fig. 19. *Outline of the delta area of the Rhine in 1300 and 1950. The proposed dams are marked.*

problem was viewed in a very different way. Fig. 19 (lower map) shows that by means of building dams near the northern and eastern entrances of the channel between North Beveland and the other islands, about 33 miles of sea wall was replaced by 2¼

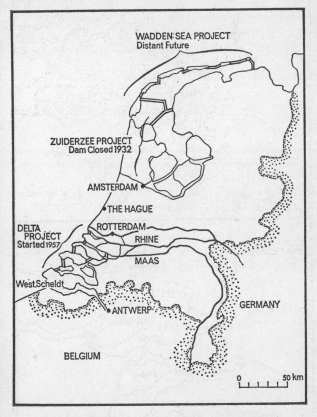

Fig. 20. *Man's influence on the coast of Holland.*

miles, although, of course, the existing sea walls must be kept in a high state of repair as a second line of defence. These dams are now finished, and the problems of building them have helped greatly in the more formidable ones that have yet to be faced. The next major construction was the Grevelingen dam, a structure which preceded the outer dams in order to mini-mise high currents in the Zijpe and elsewhere when only one of the major outer dams is completed. This dam was completed in 1963. The third important operation was the damming of the Volkerak, a rather more complicated structure since it involves a dam from a semi-artificial control island to Overflakkee, a dam and important locks between the central island and North Brabant and also a bridge over the Haringvliet to connect with Rotterdam.

The three major dams (Fig. 19) will join North Beveland and Schouwen, Schouwen to Overflakee, and Overflakee to Voorne. The engineering difficulties are formidable; not only must the dams be constructed so as to be able to withstand the most violent storms in the North Sea, but that across the Haringvliet has to allow for the discharge of fresh water from the Rhine and Meuse, and in severe winters of great quantities of ice. It will be appreciated that the siting of these dams has only been determined after the most detailed and careful work carried out in the Hydrological Laboratory at Delft. The building of these dams implies other considerable changes; the small ports on the estuary will cease to function and in some places a remunerative shell-fish industry will disappear. On the other hand the gains in fresh water, and the possibility of recreation are greatly increased, and the shortening and con-sequent improvement in the safety of the coast are enormous assets. Rotterdam and Antwerp will still be reached by the Rotterdam Waterway and the Western Scheldt. The roads and other communications in Zeeland will be vastly improved, and horticulture may well be extended. Finally, if in the course of time the slow sinking of Holland lowers the new dams too much, it will be relatively easy to raise and strengthen them, and the older walls around the existing islands will still be there as secondary defence works.

At some future time the Dutch propose another extensive reclamation, namely to take in the Wadden Sea, the shallow water area between the Frisian Islands and the mainland. (Fig. 20). If this is done almost the whole coast of the Netherlands will be defended or enclosed. No other country in the world will have increased its area to such an extent.

In this country various enclosure schemes have been adumbrated. The best known is that of Morecambe Bay. A good deal of careful work on the effect of such a barrage has been done, and at some stage, if the proposal is accepted, detailed experimental work on the hydrological problems involved must be carried out. A road across the mouth of the bay would have obvious advantages for access to west Cumberland; the enclosure of a lake of fresh water would have great economic value and would at the same time make Grange-over-Sands and other places lake-front towns and not subject as they now are to a large tidal range so that for much of each day the sea is a very long way from them. The Dee estuary would be comparatively easy to enclose; it is already very nearly filled by natural accretion and salt-marsh. A road either across the mouth, or a little way in the estuary would have an enormous effect on the interrelation of Lancashire and North Wales. A barrage across the Solway Firth, possibly along or near the line of the old railway viaduct, would enclose an extensive area of fresh water. None of these three schemes is likely to present such problems as the main dams in the Delta Plan. A much more problematical and difficult scheme is the enclosure of the Wash. The Wash is today the unfilled part of the former Fenland gulf. Natural accretion and reclamation by the building of sea walls have been continuous for centuries, and are still going on. A barrage from somewhere south of Hunstanton to the Lincolnshire coast in the neighbourhood of Wainfleet is a possibility. But would the gain of a large fresh-water lake be of greater advantage than the slower, but continuous growth of silt-land for agricultural purposes? Moreover in the Wash the problem is not just that of a barrage but also one of allowing and maintaining proper access to King's Lynn, Wisbech and other ports, and for getting rid of excess water from the fenland rivers. Advocates for the scheme claim that it would provide more than 600 million gallons a day for water supplies, and that it would improve communication and prevent flooding and the seepage of salt

into the ground. This kind of problem does not arise in the
other three cases. Whatever may be the decision on these
possible barrages, extensive planning and experimental work
must be done. The many new techniques which have been
used in coastal problems will help in various ways, and the full
repercussions of each and every scheme must be worked out.
There are also in Great Britain many other smaller estuaries
and inlets which might be enclosed, but there are also many
other interests to be considered, not least the amenities of a
coast that is already used to excess.

# 8. Use and Abuse of the Coast

In the previous chapters of this book emphasis has been laid upon the scientific aspects of coastal study. It is not inappropriate in a short final chapter to call attention to other matters. In recent years the coasts of most countries have become more and more popular as places in which to spend holidays. In what may be called railway days, before the First World War, and a few years after it, the development of the coast meant mainly the development and growth of seaside towns. It was the heyday of the hotel and boarding house visit. As the number of cars began noticeably to increase before the Second World War, people were beginning to explore the undeveloped parts of the coast and to make more use of the caravan and camping type of holiday. But after the end of petrol rationing following the war of 1939–45 – apart from the temporary break during the Suez crisis – the ever-increasing number of cars has presented many countries with not only an increasing traffic problem, but also a difficult coastal problem.

Until the Planning Acts came into force in 1947 it was possible to build houses close to the coast of this country, in places where the owners were really the sole gainers; the coastal walker might find his way blocked along cliff or beach paths, but even so the problem was not a serious one. During the two wars, but particularly in the second one, many defence and other service establishments were built on the coast, and rights of way were obstructed. Even now some of these remain, and several fine stretches of coast are only partially open to the public. On the other hand, planning authorities have usually taken care to preserve their coast, and the building of houses in coastal areas is for the most part conscientiously controlled.

But caravan and other camping sites became more and more popular in the 1950s, and legislation failed to control their expansion in many places. It soon became clear that unless some comprehensive view was taken a great deal of the coast would be spoiled, and that the very people who wanted to enjoy the coast would find themselves frustrated. Successive governments took an increasing – but often insufficient – interest in the problem. On the other hand unofficial and official bodies both began to extend their activity in regard to coastal preservation. We are particularly fortunate in having in Great Britain many trusts, national and local, interested in the coast. The National Trust, long before the initiation of Enterprise Neptune, possessed many fine coastal sites. Local county trusts following largely the lead given by the Norfolk Naturalists Trust, have become possessed of parts of the coast – Spurn Head, Gibraltar Point (Lincolnshire) and extensive parts of the Norfolk marshland coasts are examples. In 1967 the National Trust launched Enterprise Neptune, and by its means has acquired a great deal more of the coast. But official bodies have also done much, and it is only too easy to underrate their enterprise. The Nature Conservancy, now an integral part of the National Environment Research Council, is concerned with places of scientific value, and among its many nature reserves, a number are on the coast. It is, by charter, concerned only with the scientific attributes of a place, but fortunately science and amenity are by no means unrelated! It is interesting to note, for example, that Scolt Head Island, perhaps the finest reserve in the country for the study of coastal physiography, ecology, and ornithology on a low coast, was first acquired by the Norfolk Trust, and then handed to the National Trust, who have leased it to the Nature Conservancy. The National Parks Commission has also played an important part in coastal preservation. It is now replaced by the Countryside Commission. This body may own land; the original Commission could not. Nevertheless, by its influence and with the help of the wide knowledge of the land of England and Wales possessed by its members and small staff, it was able to demarcate parts of the coast, and adjoining inland country, as National Parks or Areas of Outstanding National Beauty. Shortly before its change of status the Government asked the Commission to examine the whole coast. This it has done; a series of nine regional meetings was held with the local authorities concerned, and nine reports have been published of these meetings and the discussions that took place at them, and finally an overall report will be issued and recommendations made on which it is hoped that the Government will take effective and speedy action. Apart from these national approaches, it is all important to realise that the planning authorities, the County Councils and County Borough Councils, have in many places done admirable work in clearing disfigurements of one sort or another from the coast. It is true that it can be argued that in some instances they should not have allowed caravan or other sites in the first place, but equally true that few if any, were able to foresee the expansion that took place subsequently. As it is, many councils are now spending both money and energy in clearing up a number of eyesores. Careful planning, or re-planning, can accommodate the coastal visitors without, at the same time, spoiling the coast.

There are many other demands on the coastline – harbours and shipping, industry, the expansion of existing towns, the building of nuclear power stations and the gas concessions associated with the supplies found in the North Sea. All these are right and proper demands, but collectively they mean that more and more of the natural coast is being used up. Moreover, we are all too familiar with the possibility of a disaster such as that of the *Torrey Canyon*. It is not proposed to argue the pros and cons of coastal preservation and the economic uses of the coast, but only to draw attention to the problem, a problem that is always becoming more acute. Any of the demands mentioned above, and there are others, imply better roads and access to the coast, and therefore an ever-increasing number of cars able to reach the coast. The estimated population of England and Wales in 1967 was 48½ million; the length of the coast is some 2,400 miles. A simple sum will show how many *inches* each person could have if they all wanted to visit the coast at the same time! Preservation of amenity and economic use of the coast are both necessary, but are we willing to maintain as much as possible of the coast in a natural condition? The population continues to increase; the number of cars multiplies, the demands for wider recreation in the form of marinas and small-boat sailing facilities are greater every year. The pressure on beaches, especially south of Morecambe Bay and the Tees estuary, is often excessive, and in the height of the season local country roads behind the coast in many places face traffic problems as serious as those in the narrow streets of an ancient but thriving city or market town.

The astonishing fact remains that with all these pressures there is still much unspoiled coast. Beaches may be crowded in summer, but for most of the year they are almost unused, and their beauty remains. Miles of beautiful cliffs are unspoiled and are likely to remain so. But they are being made more accessible by the construction of cliff paths so that walkers can obtain a far better appreciation of our very varied cliff scenery than was possible even a few years ago. At the same time those less able to walk are given access to many parts of the coast so that they can see an increasing amount of it and appreciate its nature. In Scotland and Ireland pressures are far less, partly because of much smaller population, partly, especially in Scotland, because of the climate. Yet even in these countries there is locally much disfigurement.

The problems with which we are faced in Britain are not peculiar to us. All countries in areas where a coastal holiday is desirable are in a similar position, but how many of them have faced the problem as we have done? How much of the French Riviera coast is open to the public? Private ownership in the United States cuts off many coastal areas, and the low sandy islands which make up much of their east coast are all too easily spoiled. The Pacific coast is beautiful, but it is being built up at an alarming rate. Australia has thousands of miles of coast, but in the east it is surprising how much is already used, and not necessarily to the best advantage. Hundreds of miles of mangrove coast in Australia and other continents are unsuitable for holiday purposes, and so, in the long run cause increased pressure elsewhere. Private ownership of the coast is increasing in the Bahamas and other tropical islands. Of course, there are still thousands of miles of natural coast in the more accessible areas of the world that are still untouched, but the lessons of certain European countries and of the United States are not readily appreciated where pressures are still minimal. A time will come, and not too distantly, in Great Britain and some other countries when it must be decided how much of the coast can be used for amenity and scientific purposes and how much for economic ends. Despite all that has happened, and is happening, on our own coast, there is no doubt that we have given a lead to the world of which we may be justifiably proud.

# Further Reading

BIRD, E. C. F. 1959. *Coastal landforms*. Australian National University, Canberra.

GUILCHER, A. 1958. *Coastal and submarine morphology*. Translated from the French by B. W. Sparks and R. H. W. Kneese. Methuen, London.

JOHNSON, D. W. 1925. *The New England—Acadian shoreline*. New York.

KING, C. A. M. 1959. *Beaches and coasts*. Arnold, London.

LINGSMA, J. S. 1963. *Holland and the Delta Plan*. Rotterdam and The Hague.

SISSONS, J. B. 1967. *The evolution of Scotland's scenery*. Oliver & Boyd, Edinburgh.

STEERS, J. A. 1962. *The sea coast*, 3rd edition. Collins, London.

STEERS, J. A. 1964. *The coastline of England and Wales*. Cambridge University Press, London.

WILLIAMS, W. W. 1960. *Coastal changes*. Routledge & Kegan Paul, London.

ZENKOVICH, V. P. *Processes of coastal development*. Translated from the Russian by D. G. Fry; edited by J. A. Steers and C. A. M. King. Oliver & Boyd, Edinburgh.

# Index

*Other titles in this series
from Oliver and Boyd
are described on the following pages*

# THE INTERIOR PLANETS
## V. A. Firsoff

Here is a critical presentation of the most up-to-date information about the Interior Planets, Mercury and Venus, following the recent successful probes of the latter.

The historical aspect is touched upon lightly, more particularly in the case of the hypothetical third Interior Planet, Vulcan, and the emphasis is on the present situation. Nevertheless, older observation work has not lost its value through the development of new techniques, and in the case of, say, the transits of Venus which will not recur this century, the observed effects retain their original interest undiminished. It is the author's view that some hypotheses, especially in the case of the physical condition of the surface and atmosphere of Venus, appear to have been overhasty as well as extreme, and cannot be easily reconciled with the totality of the observational data and what is otherwise known about the planets of the Solar System.

**Val Axel Firsoff** is the author of numerous scientific books and papers and has lectured widely to universities and societies on astronomical subjects. He is also the author of CSP 2: Life, Mind and Galaxies, published in 1967.

# EXPLORATION OF THE MOON BY SPACECRAFT

## Zdeněk Kopal

Astronomy is one of the oldest sciences conceived by the human mind, but from time immemorial has been debarred from the status of a genuine experimental science by the outer remoteness of the objects of its study. The dramatic emergence of long-range rockets in recent years has changed this time-honoured picture, at least in the inner precincts of the Solar System, and, in particular, as regards the Moon.

The aim of this volume is to focus attention on recent contributions to the study of our only natural satellite, the Moon. These contributions were made possible through parallel advances in several branches of contemporary technology – rocket propulsion, long-range radio and television transmission, electronic computer control. The author describes the actual types of spacecraft used in recent years for exploratory purposes, and he describes the results obtained with their aid and integrates them with the rest of our ground-based knowledge so as to build up a coherent picture of lunar surface environments. The concluding chapter is a prologue to manned exploration of the Moon.

**Zdeněk Kopal** is Professor of Astronomy, University of Manchester. He is the author of numerous original papers and books on astronomy, aerodynamics and applied mathematics. He is currently consultant to the Boeing Scientific Research Laboratories, Seattle, Washington. Since 1960 he has collaborated extensively with the U.S. Air Force in the mapping of the lunar surface and in other branches of lunar research.